CHICAGO PUBLIC LIBRARY

W9-AXC-288

CHICAGO PUBLIC LIBRARY
CLEARING BRANCH
6423 WEST 63RD PLACE
CHICAGO, ILLINOIS 60638-5005

Chicago Public Library

REFERENCE

Form 178 rev. 1-94

The Encyclopedia of
North American Indians

Volume V

Georgia – Inuit

General Editor
D. L. Birchfield

Marshall Cavendish
New York • London • Toronto

Contents

R01605 43132

CHICAGO PUBLIC LIBRARY
CLEARING BRANCH
6423 W. 63RD PL.   60638

Published in 1997 by
Marshall Cavendish Corporation
99 White Plains Road
Tarrytown, NY 10591-9001
U.S.A.

© 1997 by Marshall Cavendish Corporation

Developed, designed, and produced by Water Buffalo Books, Milwaukee

All rights reserved.
No part of this book may be reproduced or utilized in any form or by any means, electronic
or mechanical, including photocopying, recording, or by any information storage and
retrieval system, without prior written permission from the publisher and copyright holder.

Project director: Mark J. Sachner
General editor: D. L. Birchfield
Art director: Sabine Beaupré
Photo researcher: Diane Laska
Project editor: Valerie J. Weber

Editors: Elizabeth Kaplan, MaryLee Knowlton, Judith Plumb, Carolyn Kott Washburne

Consulting editors: Donna Beckstrom, Jack D. Forbes, Annette Reed Crum, John Bierhorst

Picture credits: © 1995 Paul Abdoo: 629; © B. & C. Alexander: 613, 614, 615, 620, 717, 719, 720; © Archive Photos: 584,
663, 676, 681, 703; © Archive Photos/American Stock: 597, 598, 647; © Archive Photos/Hirz: 609; ASUCLA Photo by
Terry O'Donneli: 644; Sabine Beaupré 1996: 650, 700; © Steve Bly: 685; © Kit Breen: 667, 702, 704, 710; © Brown Brothers,
Sterling, PA: 589; © Corbis-Bettmann: 582, 585, 586, 587, 617 (top), 627, 646, 648, 662; © Culver Pictures: 619; © Steven
Ferry: 706; © Eugene Fisher: 656, 718; © Robert Frerck, Odyssey Productions: 640, 690, 691, 692, 693, 696; © Judith Gish: 591;
Beryl Goldberg, Photographer © 1995: 651; Courtesy of Raven Hail: 623; © Hampton University Archives, Hampton, Virginia:
625, 626; Courtesy of Barbara and Geary Hobson: 653; Courtesy of LeAnne Howe: 677; © James Humphries, Choctaw Nation of
Oklahoma: 606; © '94 Millie Knapp: 605; © Dan Marshall Photography: 593; © Kevin O. Mooney, Odyssey Productions: 687;
© Tom Myers Photography 1995: 684; © Leslie M. Newman: Cover, 673; The Philbrook Museum of Art, Tulsa, Oklahoma: 610;
© Margaret Randall: 602; © Susan Silberberg: 655; State Historical Society of Wisconsin, neg. #WHi(X3)45637: 660; © STOCK
MONTAGE, INC.: 581, 617 (bottom); © Richard Strauss, Smithsonian Institution: 611; © Stephen Trimble: title, 592, 601, 633,
634, 635, 636, 657, 659, 666, 668, 669, 670, 671, 675 (both), 678, 679, 682, 689, 707 (both), 712, 715, 716; © Robert J. Turney:
642; © UPI/Corbis-Bettmann: 621, 631, 637, 638, 698, 701

Library of Congress Cataloging-in-Publication Data

The encyclopedia of North American Indians.
     p. cm.
     Includes bibliographical references and index.
     Summary: A comprehensive reference work on the culture and history of Native Americans.
     ISBN 0-7614-0232-2 (vol. 5)   ISBN 0-7614-0227-6 (lib. bdg.: set)
     1. Indians of North America--Encyclopedias, Juvenile.
    [1. Indians of North America--Encyclopedias.]
    E76.2.E53   1997
    970.004'97'003--dc20
                                                      96-7700
                                                      CIP
                                                      AC

Printed and bound in Italy

Title page illustration: A Hopi seed jar, crafted by contemporary Hopi potter Dextra Quotskuyva.

Editor's note: Many systems of dating have been used by different cultures throughout history.
The Encyclopedia of North American Indians uses B.C.E. (Before Common Era) and C.E. (Common Era)
instead of B.C. (Before Christ) and A.D. (Anno Domini, "In the Year of the Lord") out of respect
for the diversity of the world's peoples.

GEORGIA

Georgia became a U.S. state when it ratified the U.S. Constitution along with the other original thirteen colonies. The state of Georgia has many connections to American Indians.

There is evidence of Indians having lived in present-day Georgia for a long time. Some archaeologists have studied the material culture of inhabitants in the area from a period dating to within a few hundred years before European contact. From 1925 through 1928, the Etowah Mounds—located near present-day Cartersville—were excavated. Many items were unearthed, including copper axes, engraved copper and shells, stone figurines, and stone coffins. The Etowah Mounds were part of a fortified village complex, which was occupied between 1200 and 1700 C.E. It is believed that the Etowah people are directly related to the Cherokee and Creek people.

Hernando de Soto was the first European to travel in the area now known as Georgia, when he crossed the region in 1539–1540. The first European settlement in Georgia was Savannah, which was established in 1733 by James Oglethorpe.

Oglethorpe was a British general and member of Parliament who secured a charter for a colony in Georgia from King George II. Oglethorpe set up the colony as a sanctuary for the English poor, but it also served as an outpost against Spanish incursions from Florida.

At the time the English started invading Georgia, there were two major tribes living in the area. To the north were the Cherokees, and in the south lived the Creeks (also known as the Muscogee Confederation). The English invasion of the interior of the state was opposed by these two tribes, and it took seven decades to take the Cherokee and Creek homelands. By 1826, the last of the Creek land was seized, and by 1838, the last of the Cherokee land was lost.

There are currently no federal reservations in Georgia and no federally recognized tribes in the state. There is one state-recognized tribe, however, the Tama. The 1990 U.S. Census lists 13,348 Indians as Georgia residents, placing Georgia thirtieth among U.S. states in Native American population.

SEE ALSO:
De Soto Expedition.

James Oglethorpe, the British military man and lawmaker who established the first European settlement in Georgia at present-day Savannah, is greeted by his Native hosts during their first encounter in the early 1730s.

GERMAN SETTLERS

After the British, the Germans are the largest immigrant group in the United States. From the time of the voyages of Columbus, German interest in North America has remained high. In 1507, the mapmaker Martin Waldseemuller suggested the name *America* for the "new" continent. In 1520, Albrecht Dürer, artist and goldsmith, marveled at Aztec artifacts that had been sent to Emperor Charles V. Through the centuries, German writers have published numerous books about North America and its original people. Sometimes they portrayed it as "waste country" full of "lurking Indians"; sometimes they painted it as a land of plenty where "noble savages" could be saved by Christian intervention. Settlers were often guided by the same images.

Serious German immigration did not begin until the late 1600s, but Germans came to North America at least as early as 1607. John Smith of Jamestown Colony lists several German ("Dutch")

craftsmen among the original settlers. Some of them were ordered by Smith to build a house for Wahunsonacock, chief of the Powhatan Confederacy, in return for food supplies. Realizing the difficult situation of the colony—the lack of food and disagreements among the settlers—the Germans decided to stay with the Powhatans, whom they considered more powerful, and to tell Wahunsonacock about Smith's needs and projects for the survival and growth of Jamestown.

A Dutchman with German ties, Peter Minuit, became the first governor of New Netherland. Unlike Spanish explorers or British traders, who took possession of the regions they entered, Minuit bought Manhattan Island from the Indians. Other early Germans were explorers or adventurers, among them John Lederer, who from 1669 to 1670 investigated the Carolinas and relied on Indian guides.

The first major group of German immigrants, the Mennonites, arrived in Pennsylvania in 1683. They were religious refugees and had been invited by the English Quaker William Penn. In Pennsyl-

Peter Minuit negotiates the purchase of Manhattan Island with local Native leaders. Minuit, whose name was also spelled *Minnwit,* was the German-born first director (governor) of the Dutch New Netherland colony.

vania, they settled on land bought from Penn, who, in turn, had purchased it from the Delawares. Other religious groups followed, among them the Amish and Moravians. Like the Quakers, these groups objected to war and violence, even in cases of self-defense. They dealt with Indians honestly and respectfully. Most of the Germans objected to slavery, black or red. Hardworking, with large families in which even the women did field labor, these farmers did not need indentured Indian servants either.

The Moravians called the Indians their "brothers and sisters" and sought to convert them to Christianity. Moravian missionaries in Pennsylvania learned the Delaware language, established Christian Indian communities, and attempted to indoctrinate the Indians in European agricultural practices, crafts, and religion. They did not approve of marriages between the races and expelled a missionary who had married a Delaware woman.

After 1700, war and persecution at home forced many Germans to seek a new life overseas. They settled in New York, Pennsylvania, Maryland, New Jersey, Virginia, the Carolinas, Georgia, and New England. Supposedly, one group of exiled Germans who stopped over in London aroused the pity of some Mohawk chiefs then visiting Queen Mary. The chiefs offered them land for purchase in the Mohawk Valley. Once settled there, the German settlers and the Mohawks established friendly relations. The Mohawks helped the Germans through their first winter, the two groups participated in each other's festivals, and at least one family sent their son to live among the Mohawks to learn their language and customs.

The peaceful cooperation between German settlers and Indians came to an end during the wars of the late eighteenth century: the French and Indian War, 1756–1763; Pontiac's War, 1763–1765; and the American Revolution, 1775–1783. German settlers, who often farmed along the border of a colony, were caught in the crossfire of the warring European nations and their Indian allies. They suffered great losses in lives and goods, and many joined the public opinion that all Indians were "bad." In Pennsylvania, even the pacifist Moravians felt forced to distinguish between "good Indians" and "savages." Increasing tension and anti-Indian feelings led to massacres of Christian Indians in Pennsylvania in 1762 and at Gnadenhutten, Ohio, in 1782.

During the wars, some Germans were kidnapped by Indians to replace a member of the tribe. On their return from captivity, often years later, some of them wrote narratives that described the hardships they had suffered. Some Germans became ruthless Indian fighters whose only goal in life was to avenge the death of family members by killing as many Indians as possible.

As German immigration grew, Germans followed the westward-moving frontier and settled in Ohio, Kentucky, and Tennessee. They founded towns in Wisconsin, Michigan, Minnesota, and Texas. German settlers also appeared in California, Oregon, and Washington. Some of them still belonged to religious groups whose faith outlawed violence, such as the Moravians and Mennonites mentioned earlier. Their missionary work among the different tribes, including the Cherokees, Comanches, Cheyennes, and Arapahos, allowed them to see the Indians' desperate situation at firsthand. Among the Moravian missionaries, several criticized the government's removal policy; the Mennonites often sided with the Indians against the ever-increasing numbers of pioneers.

The rest of the Germans, however, differed little from immigrants of other nationalities. In search of land, most settlers saw Indians as hostiles who interfered with their farming and way of life rather than as patriots defending the invasion of their country. If they acknowledged at all that the Indians' grievances were justified, they could not understand why the Indians did not always distinguish between "good" and "bad" whites and instead raided all settlers alike. The settlers themselves, of course, were also unwilling to make the difference between "good" and "bad" Indians.

Little Crow's War of 1862, in which the Santee Sioux fought back against the theft of monies and goods by Indian agents and traders, serves as an example. Calling it a massacre, not a war, the U.S. military did not distinguish between warriors and criminals and initially sentenced 303 Sioux to die. Citizens of New Ulm, the German settlement that had been attacked during the war, sought "private revenge" against the Sioux by attacking prisoners with pitchforks, boiling water, and stones as the prisoners were being transferred to a different camp.

Over the course of his political career, Carl Schurz promoted and helped implement U.S. government policy in the areas of Indian removal, allotment, and forced boarding school education. He also helped the government implement its policies in the South during the era of Reconstruction following the Civil War.

Several prisoners were hurt. Their execution was delayed until President Abraham Lincoln could examine the death sentences. In the end, Lincoln confirmed the death penalty for 39 Sioux; the others were shipped off to prison.

To round out the account of German settlers and their interactions and relations with Indians, several German individuals who greatly influenced Indians' lives need to be mentioned. One of these was Conrad Weiser (1696–1760), who as a youth gained inside knowledge of Mohawk language and culture. As respected interpreter and Indian agent of Pennsylvania to the Iroquois Confederacy during the years leading up to the French and Indian War, Weiser attended numerous council and treaty meetings and helped settle many difficult situations.

Another German, John Jacob Astor (1763–1848), founder of the American Fur Company, played a major role in changing the lives of Indians by making them dependent on European goods. In addition, his trading centers, where alcohol was sold freely, encouraged drinking among Indians and shut down the alcohol-free government trading posts. Finally, Secretary of the Interior Carl Schurz (1829–1906) continued the Indian Removal Policy, promoted allotment, and supported forceful education of Indian children away from the reservations in schools such as the Carlisle Indian School in Pennsylvania.

— H. Z. Weidner

SEE ALSO:

Boarding Schools; Colonialism; European Attitudes Toward Indigenous Peoples; General Allotment Act; Removal Act, Indian; Pennsylvania.

GERONIMO (1829–1909)

The man who would become known as Geronimo was born in what is now the state of Arizona about 1829. He was born into the Bedonkohe band of the Chiricahua Apaches, a tribe of Arizona and northern Mexico (now divided between the Apaches of Fort Sill, Oklahoma, and the Mescalero Apaches of New Mexico), and his name was Gokhlayeh (sometimes spelled Goyathlay). When he was seventeen years old, he was admitted into the Council of Warriors. He married, and he and his wife had three children.

In 1858, when Gokhlayeh was twenty-nine years old, he and his family went with the people of his band on a trip to Mexico to trade. They set up their camp, and the men went into a town to trade. While they were gone, Mexican soldiers attacked the camp, killing women and children, including Gokhlayeh's family.

Later, seeking revenge for the atrocity committed against his loved ones, Gokhlayeh visited the great Cochise to ask him to join a raid into Mexico. Cochise agreed, and in the summer of 1859, three bands of Apaches went into Mexico. On the day of the big battle, Gokhlayeh was given the honor of leading the Apaches. Under his leadership, the Apaches were victorious. During and after this battle, the Mexicans called Gokhlayeh by the name *Geronimo*. (Some say that when fright-

When Geronimo posed for this photo around 1895, he was a prisoner of war at Fort Sill, Oklahoma, about ten years after he surrendered to U.S. forces in Arizona.

ened Mexican soldiers saw Gokhlayeh charging, they called out for protection from St. Jerome, whose name in Spanish is *Geronimo*.) From that time on, Gokhlayeh would remain a bitter enemy of the Mexicans, and he would be forever known as Geronimo.

Not satisfied with this act of revenge, Geronimo led another raid into Mexico the following summer with only twenty-five men. This time, he was wounded in the battle by a blow to the head with a rifle butt. The next summer, with only twelve men, he went again. This time he was wounded twice, and the raid was unsuccessful. Geronimo was blamed for the failure by the people of his band.

At last the Mexicans retaliated, sending three companies of soldiers across the border to raid Geronimo's village. A few warriors were killed along with a large number of women and children. These raids back and forth across the border would continue throughout most of Geronimo's life.

In 1861, when Geronimo was thirty-two years old, a new war began, this one with the United States. A white man named Ward, married to an Indian woman, had beaten his own son. The boy, who was half Indian, fled to Cochise for protection. Ward then accused Cochise of having kidnapped the boy and stolen some livestock. The U.S. Army chose to believe Ward, and Cochise was arrested, along with five members of his family.

Cochise managed to escape, and he captured some white people to exchange for his relatives. Lieutenant George Bascom, in charge of the situation, refused the exchange. Cochise's white captives were killed, and Cochise's relatives were hanged. Thus began a long and bloody war between the United States and the Apaches. It would last for over twenty years.

While other Apache leaders moved with their people onto reservations in order to avoid the violence, Cochise and another Chiricahua leader, Mangas Colorado, continued the fight. Eventually, Mangas Colorado was murdered under a flag of truce,

Geronimo (bottom row, third from right), and other Apache prisoners, in 1886, seated on a hillside in Arizona outside the railroad cars that would take them to prison in Florida.

Late in life, Geronimo was frequently photographed in settings that seemed to be in great contrast to the Indian wars of the late nineteenth century. Here, in 1908, about a year before his death, while still a prisoner of war, he is sitting at the wheel of an automobile.

and, in his sixties, Cochise at last agreed to settle on a reservation.

By 1877, Geronimo and his followers were among the few who had not moved onto the reservations. Word was sent to him to come in for a talk with U.S. government officials. He did, and he was arrested, put in irons, and kept in prison for four months. He was released onto the San Carlos Reservation.

Conditions were bad at San Carlos, and several Native leaders attempted to lead their people to freedom away from the reservation. One such leader, Victorio, and his followers left San Carlos. He fought both the U.S. and the Mexicans for the next two years but was killed in Mexico in 1880. Nana, at the age of seventy, had also led his people off San Carlos. Rumors were spread on the reservation that Geronimo was to be hanged. In 1881, followed by about seventy warriors, he left San Carlos and crossed the border into Mexico. He was fifty-two years old.

Geronimo and his followers later returned to San Carlos in an attempt to recruit others to join them. On their return trip to Mexico with most of the Mescaleros and many Warm Springs Apaches, they were attacked by U.S. soldiers. Attempting to protect the women and children, the Apache men stayed behind to fight, but Mexican soldiers then attacked from the other direction, killing most of the women and children. Geronimo and the other survivors went on into Mexico to join up with Nana.

U.S. General George Crook assumed command at San Carlos in 1882 and the following year managed to arrange a meeting with Geronimo in Mexico. He agreed with Geronimo that the Apaches had been treated badly on the reservation and promised that things would be better. Geronimo agreed to return. By 1884, he was back at San Carlos.

For some reason, *Geronimo* was the name that was known to all the non-Indian people of the Southwest, and even though Indian raids in Arizona and New Mexico had been led by Chato, Nana, Chihuahua, and others, most of the raids had been attributed to Geronimo. With such notoriety attached to his name, Geronimo became even more feared—and hated—by non-Indians. Once again he became the object of rumors spread throughout the reservation, and once again, these rumors concerned his impending death by hanging. It was even said that if the army failed to do the job, non-Indian civilian vigilantes were prepared to take over and lynch him.

In the summer of 1885, believing the rumors to be true or at least plausible, Geronimo cut the telegraph wires to San Carlos and left the reservation with ninety-two women and children and thirty-four men. Before reaching Mexico, some of his people, led by Chihuahua, changed their minds and decided to return to San Carlos. On their way back, they were attacked by U.S. Cavalry. Chihuahua led a series of raids in retaliation, and once again, Geronimo received the blame.

In 1886, General Crook began what would be his final campaign against Geronimo. He again met with Geronimo and convinced him to surrender and return to the reservation. On his way back to San Carlos, however, Geronimo had second thoughts. He turned back toward Mexico. Following this failure to return Geronimo to the reservation, Crook was reprimanded. He eventually resigned and was replaced by General Nelson Miles.

Miles went after Geronimo with five thousand soldiers and five hundred Apache scouts. By this time, Geronimo's entire force numbered only twenty-four men. Thousands of civilian militia joined the pursuit, as did, south of the border, thousands of Mexican Army troops. Geronimo eluded them all throughout the summer of 1886.

At last, U.S. Lieutenant Charles Gatewood and two Apache scouts located Geronimo. After a talk with Gatewood, Geronimo agreed to talk to Miles, and at last, he surrendered to Miles. From San Carlos, he was taken to San Antonio, Texas, and held in jail for forty days. There was a serious attempt to try him for murder in civilian courts, and the voice of President Grover Cleveland joined those who were calling for Geronimo to be hanged.

Instead of being hanged, Geronimo was taken to Florida, where he was imprisoned at Fort Pickens, while the main body of the Chiricahua tribe was held at Fort Marion, Florida, to serve time at hard labor. After two years, they were transferred to Mount Vernon Barracks, Alabama. In 1894, they were sent to Fort Sill, in what is now Oklahoma. In 1898, when Geronimo was sixty-nine years old, he was finally excused from any more hard labor.

In 1904, still a prisoner of war but also the subject of interest and curiosity as a veteran of wars against both the United States and Mexico, Geronimo was escorted to the World's Fair in St. Louis by members of the Indian Bureau. The following year, he rode in the inauguration parade of President Theodore Roosevelt. Throughout these years, he begged to be allowed to return to Arizona. But it was not to be.

Also in 1905, S. M. Barrett, superintendent of schools in Lawton, Oklahoma, received permission to interview Geronimo in order to write the old man's "autobiography." Over a period of time and a succession of interviews, Geronimo told his story in Apache to Asa Daklugie, who translated it into English for Barrett to write down. Then, at Geronimo's insistence, Barrett read aloud what he had written, and Daklugie translated it back into Apache for Geronimo's final approval. The result was Geronimo's *Story of His Life*, published in 1907 by Duffield and Company. The book has been reprinted several times.

Still trying to get permission to return to Arizona, Geronimo tactfully omitted telling anything about fights with the United States, concentrating instead on his battles with the Mexican Army, and he dedicated the book to President Roosevelt. It did not help. He died at Fort Sill in 1909, nearly eighty years old and still a prisoner of war.

— R. J. Conley

SEE ALSO:

Apache; Cochise; Crook, George; San Carlos Reservation; Victorio.

SUGGESTED READINGS:

Debo, Angie. *Geronimo*. Norman: University of Oklahoma Press, 1979.

Roberts, David. *Once They Moved Like the Wind: Cochise, Geronimo, and the Apache Wars*. New York: Simon and Schuster, 1993.

Worchester, Donald E. *Apaches: Eagles of the Southwest*. Norman: University of Oklahoma Press, 1979.

GHOST DANCE RELIGION

The Ghost Dance religion grew out of a vision had by Wovoka, a Paiute prophet from Pyramid Lake, Nevada, while he was employed as a sheepherder for a white rancher. During a solar eclipse on New Year's Day in 1889, Wovoka fell seriously ill, became delirious, and experienced a vision in which he was taken up to heaven. In his vision, Wovoka saw all the dead people of his tribe happy, alive again, and at peace. When Wovoka awoke, he told of being instructed by God to tell his people to cease fighting and regain peace. He was told to teach them special prayers, songs, and a new dance. If his people practiced these things, their dead relatives and friends would come back to life, buffalo would cover the lands again, all the whites would disappear, and the Indians' homelands would once again be theirs.

At the time of Wovoka's vision, Indian tribes were suffering from a great many misfortunes. What were once strong and proud nations had within just a few short years undergone a series of terrible tragedies and were in a state of despair. Thousands of Indian people had died at the hands of non-Indian soldiers and settlers, and many more were sick from diseases and poor living conditions. Indians were ordered off their homelands and forced to live on reservations, where their traditional ways were seriously threatened. Wovoka's gospel came to the people during perhaps one of the darkest times of their history, and many tribes were desperately searching for salvation. His message offered the Indians something to believe in, and it inspired faith and hope during a time when it seemed that all had been lost.

Wovoka's messianic religion quickly spread across the Plains, from tribe to tribe, and soon the Kiowas, Cheyennes, Arapahos, and Comanches were performing the rituals, songs, and dances of the Ghost Dance. The Sioux also had heard the promise of a religion that would resurrect the world to the way things had been before the coming of the whites, and exalted by the message that they could dance a new world into being, the Sioux sent two messengers to learn more from the Paiute holy man, Wovoka.

These messengers were Kicking Bear from the Cheyenne River Reservation and Short Bull from

This drawing, by J. Steeple Davis, purports to illustrate the Ghost Dance. What it actually illustrates are prevailing non-Native attitudes about Native ceremonials.

the Rosebud Reservation. They traveled for hundreds of miles across fences and railroad tracks and through white-occupied lands, until they finally met the famed Paiute holy man. Wovoka instructed them to look into his hat, and in it, they reported, they could see the entire world reborn. They saw the Plains covered with buffalo. They saw their dead relatives and friends alive and happy again. Wovoka offered them the instructions in which to perform the Ghost Dance religion, and the messengers returned home to share with their people what they had learned.

The Sioux began to perform the Ghost Dance. They constructed special clothing, Ghost Dance shirts, which were painted with symbols of the moon, the sun, stars, crosses, eagles, and magpies. These designs were thought to make the shirts bulletproof, so the wearers would be invulnerable to the white soldiers' weapons. The dancing sometimes lasted for several days. Indian men, women, and children formed a circle and shuffled to the right and then to the left, singing and chanting. Sometimes a person would fall into a trance and experience a vision, later telling the people what he or she had seen. Some of the dancers claimed to have met Jesus, while others had gone to the spirit world and been reunited with relatives who had passed on. Some people traveled to the moon and returned clutching pieces of moon rock or powder.

Though the Ghost Dance offered Indian people many profound and mysterious experiences, it was misunderstood by white people, who found the dancing and singing threatening. Some whites thought the dance represented an uprising, an act of aggression. A Pine Ridge agent, Daniel Royer, thought the dance was hostile and sent word to Washington, D.C., for help. Agent Royer's concern resulted in the murder of the respected Hunkpapa leader, Sitting Bull, as well as the death of eight other Sioux and six policemen. But the trouble didn't end there. A few days later, nearly three hundred Sioux men, women, and children were killed by the Seventh Cavalry, at the site of Wounded Knee, on the Pine Ridge Reservation in South Dakota.

The Ghost Dance was revived in 1974 by Henry Crow Dog, whose grandfather was one of the original Ghost Dance leaders. The philosophies and teachings of the Ghost Dance have not perished. For many Indian people, the dream is still alive.

— T. Midge

SEE ALSO:

Crow Dog; Crow Dog, Henry; Kicking Bear; Sitting Bull; Wounded Knee (1890).

GIAGO, TIM (1934–)

Tim Giago, a Sioux, is the editor and publisher of *Indian Country Today* (the former *Lakota Times*), which is one of the largest Indian-owned newspapers on the North American continent. He also writes a weekly column, titled "Notes from Indian Country," which is syndicated by Knight-Ridder News Service and is carried by three hundred newspapers.

Giago was born on the Pine Ridge Reservation in South Dakota at the Indian Health Service Hospital on July 12, 1934. He attended elementary and high school at the Holy Rosary Indian Mission, now known as the Red Cloud Indian School, from 1941 to 1951. He entered the U.S. Navy in 1952, served in the Korean conflict, and obtained his general education diploma in Sasebo, Japan, in 1952. He was honorably discharged from the navy in 1958 after being awarded a Korean Ribbon with stars, a United Nations Medal, a Syngman Rhee Korean Unit Citation, a Good Conduct Medal, and a China Service Medal. Giago attended San Jose Junior College at San Jose, California, and the University of Nevada at Reno and was awarded a Niemann Fellowship to Harvard University in 1990–1991. He received an honorary doctorate of humanities from Nebraska Indian Community College in 1993.

Giago serves on the Board of Advisors for the First Amendment Center at Vanderbilt University in Nashville, Tennessee, and the National Conference of Christians and Jews in Minneapolis, Minnesota. He is also the chief executive officer and president of Native American Publishing, Inc., and founded the Native American Journalists Association in 1984 and served as its first president.

His books include *The Aboriginal Sin*, published in 1978, and a collection of his weekly newspaper columns, *Notes from Indian Country*, published in 1985. He also wrote *The American Indian and the Media* in 1993. Giago has written for *USA Today*, *The Christian Science Monitor*, *Newsweek*, *The New York Times*, and *New York Newsday*, and he has been featured in *People*, *The New York Times*, *The Wall Street Journal*, and *Minnesota Monthly* magazine, among many others. He has appeared as a guest on the "Oprah Winfrey Show," South Dakota Public Television, Christian Science Monitor Television, Canadian Broadcasting Company TV, "NBC Nightly News," and CBS's "Nightwatch."

Giago was inducted into South Dakota's Hall of Fame in October 1994. He received the Medal of Honor for Distinguished Journalism from the University of Missouri School of Journalism in 1991 and was recognized for contributions to American journalism by Harvard University in 1991. He was also honored for contributions to civil and human rights by the National Education Association in 1995, and he was Media Person of the Year for Native Americans in 1982.

SEE ALSO:

Native American Journalists Association.

In Robert Gish's collection of short stories, *First Horses: Stories of the New West*, the reader finds real people, rather than Old West stereotypes.

GISH, ROBERT F. (1940–)

Robert Franklin Gish, a Native writer of Cherokee and Choctaw heritage, is a member of the Cherokee Nation of Oklahoma. Both of his parents were born in Indian Territory. Gish was born in Albuquerque, New Mexico, on April 1, 1940. He was educated at the University of New Mexico, where he earned B.A. (1962), M.A. (1967), and Ph.D. (1972) degrees. A college teacher, Gish served as professor of English and University Distinguished Scholar at the University of Northern Iowa in Cedar Falls, Iowa, and as director of ethnic studies at California Polytechnic State University in San Luis Obispo, California.

Gish's poetry has been anthologized in *Returning the Gift: Poetry and Prose from the First North American Native Writers' Festival* (University of Arizona Press, 1994), and his short fiction has been anthologized in *Aniyunwiya/Real Human Beings: An Anthology of Contemporary Cherokee Prose* (Greenfield Review Press, 1995).

His books include *Hamlin Garland: The Far West* (Boise State University Press, 1976), *Paul Horgan* (G. K. Hall, 1983), *Frontier's End: The Life and Literature of Harvey Fergusson* (University of Nebraska Press, 1988), *William Carlos Williams: The Short Fiction* (G. K. Hall, 1989), *Songs of My Hunter Heart: A Western Kinship* (Iowa State University

Press, 1991), *First Horses: Stories of the New West* (University of Nevada Press, 1993), and *When Coyote Howls: A Lavaland Fable* (University of New Mexico Press, 1995).

In *First Horses: Stories of the New West*, which consists of fourteen original short stories, Gish recreates the multicultural complexities of Albuquerque, New Mexico, as he knew the city and its cultures during his youth in the 1950s. A number of the stories are coming of age stories, others probe political and religious hypocrisy, and others present vignettes of daily life in that time and place. The stories are distinguished for their range of subject matter and for their insights.

Gish is a member of Western Writers of America, the Screen Actors Guild, and the Author's Guild. He contributes articles and reviews to a wide range of publications, is a contributing editor to *The Bloomsbury Review*, and serves on the editorial board of *Western American Literature* and *The American Indian Culture and Research Journal*.

GIVEAWAY

The "Giveaway," a ceremony in which the host honors guests with presents, is best known among the Pacific Northwest Coast Native nations in the form of the "Potlatch." Many other Native peoples also have ceremonies that feature gift giving. In the twentieth century, the "Giveaway" has become a part of pan-Indian cultural observances in many areas.

At the time of European contact, economic, political, and ceremonial power was highly prized and unequally distributed among the Northwest Coast tribes. Like few other Native peoples, they paid intense attention to private property. Such wealth often was inherited. A chief might own a lodge, salvage rights in nearby forests, and even fishing rights along a portion of coastline for miles offshore. Chiefs also owned salmon spawning streams and the right to fish in them. A chief might also own important ceremonial property,

Giveaways are best known among Pacific Northwest peoples, but they are a part of the culture of many tribes. Here, a food giveaway is a part of an Apache girl's puberty ceremony in Whitewater, Arizona.

such as dances and songs, as well as the right to present certain rituals. Lesser chiefs owned less valuable resources; all land that had an economic use was owned by some member of the nobility. A chief could create power networks under his patronage by allowing lesser chiefs' families or commoners access to his lands and waters, usually for a second harvest.

Because the chief controlled the access of people in lower orders to food, shelter, and even spiritual sustenance, the societies of the Northwest Coast peoples were more hierarchical than even the Aztecs or the monarchial societies of Europe during the period of first contacts with Native America. There were no councils to exercise restraint on them. As noted, however, a "good chief" did gather power by being generous to those "under the arm." The ceremonial potlatch was an expression of this ethic: On one level, it was a display of wealth by the chief or chiefs hosting it; on another level, the intricate gift giving of the ritual bespoke an inherent—but, like all other aspects of Northwest Coast life, tightly controlled—distribution of that same wealth. The potlatch thus consolidated the power and authority of its hosts by reminding lesser nobles and commoners that the high chiefs controlled every aspect of village life.

Among the Northwest Coast peoples, the potlatch was not usually concerned so much with the economic goals of getting and giving as with enhancing social status, honoring ancestors, and sealing marriages. According to Duane Champagne, the ritual "should be understood from within its own cultural and institutional framework, and not be too easily compared with self-interested materialism." Similarly, the emphasis on rank in Northwest Coast societies was not simply an imitation of Western hierarchical societies. Instead, the Tlingit concept of rank was integrated into that people's belief that proper behavior in the present (such as contributing to potlatches, fulfilling one's clan obligations, and submitting to the collective will of the house group) could cause one to be reborn into a more aristocratic lineage.

Diane Glancy, recipient of the first North American Indian Prose Award, is also an accomplished playwright, novelist, and poet.

GLANCY, DIANE (1941–)

Cherokee writer Diane Glancy was born on March 18, 1941, in Kansas City, Missouri. She received a B.A. in English in 1964 from the University of Missouri, an M.A. in creative writing in 1983 from Central State University in Edmond, Oklahoma, and an M.F.A. in scripting in 1988 from the University of Iowa. She is a prolific writer working in many different genres, including poetry, fiction, nonfiction, autobiography, and plays. She teaches creative writing at Macalester College in St. Paul, Minnesota.

In 1984, when Glancy's poetry was anthologized in *Songs from This Earth on Turtle's Back* (Greenfield Review Press), and when she was completing her M.A. in creative writing, her work had already appeared in more than seventy small-press

GOLD RUSH

Gold rushes occurred frequently throughout the nineteenth century on the North American continent, and their impact on the lives of Native peoples was severe. In the southeastern portion of the continent, the southern gold rush of 1828 on the lands of the Cherokees hastened the forced removal of the so-called Five Civilized Tribes to lands west of the Mississippi River. In California, the gold rush of 1849 was devastating for Native peoples, bringing to the region lawless hordes of fortune seekers who pushed indigenous peoples out of their way, killing them with impunity.

Along the front range of the Rocky Mountains, the discovery of gold near Denver in 1859 swelled the population with the sort of men who joined Colonel John Chivington's Third Colorado Volunteers and massacred Black Kettle's peaceful band of Southern Cheyennes at Sand Creek in 1864. On the northern Great Plains, the discovery of gold in the Black Hills and the ensuing gold rush in 1876 led directly to war with the Sioux and eventually led to the confinement of the Sioux to reservations. Late in the century, the discovery of gold in Alaska brought European diseases to the far north, along with hordes of men who had no regard for the rights of indigenous peoples.

Everywhere that U.S. citizens found gold, Native peoples in those regions were soon overwhelmed. Not only did Native peoples suffer, but respect for the rule of law and for governmental institutions also suffered. Greed for gold caused United States citizens to ignore a U.S. Supreme Court decision, *Worcester v. Georgia* in 1832, which would have prevented the state of Georgia from extending its laws to the Cherokee Nation—if the decision in the case had been enforced. Rather than enforce the Supreme Court decision, Andrew Jackson, then president of the United States, forced the Cherokees to leave their ancestral homelands. In addition, their lust for gold caused United States citizens to openly violate the Treaty of Fort Laramie of 1868 with the Sioux when they poured into the Black Hills in search of gold in 1876. Rather than use the United States Army to remove the gold miners and uphold its obligations under the treaty, the United States pursued a war of conquest against the Sioux. Wherever gold was discovered, Native peoples could find no protection for their rights in the courts and no protection from their treaties.

For some unknown reason, the southern gold rush of 1828 has never attracted the attention of American historians that it deserves. It played a vital role in the history of the Indian nations in the region and for Indian relations throughout the nineteenth century, and it proved to be a crucial training ground for the men who would go to California in 1848. To a large extent, it was southerners in the California goldfields who taught the other men how to extract gold from the streambeds and who also taught the others how to disregard the rights of Indians. Because it was the first gold rush and because it set a pattern regarding Indian relations that would be repeated over and over again, the southern gold rush deserves special attention here.

The southern gold rush began as a series of small discoveries of gold along the Piedmont region of the Appalachian Mountains in North and South Carolina beginning in the late 1790s. Eventually, gold was found in seventeen counties in the Carolinas. The first recorded instance of the discovery of gold in the area occurred in Cabarrus County, North Carolina, in 1799. It was also one of the most unusual discoveries in the history of gold exploration in North America. There, a farmer's son found a seventeen-pound (nearly eight-kilogram) nugget of almost pure gold in a streambed, one of the largest nuggets ever found. The farmer sold it to a jeweler in a nearby town for $3.50, and the jeweler sold it for several thousand dollars. Soon, men were digging for gold throughout the Piedmont region, finding lots of nuggets and placer deposits (gold that had settled in streambeds), but no mother lode, as gold miners refer to a large strike.

Throughout the early 1800s, the succession of discoveries generally followed a pattern of north to south in the Piedmont region of the Carolinas, moving ever closer to the southern boundary of the Cherokee country in northern Georgia. Then, in October of 1828, in the Cherokee Nation, on land also claimed by the state of Georgia as part of Hall County (later Lumpkin County), gold prospectors stumbled upon the mother lode. By 1829, thousands of miners were flooding into the area, and towns were popping up everywhere. Some of those

A gold-mining operation at Wickenburg, Arizona. This photograph, taken in the 1880s, gives an idea of the size and scope of gold mining once it took hold in the West.

towns roared for a while and then were eventually abandoned, such as Auraria, and some of them remain today, such as Dahlonega. Eventually, Dahlonega was found to be at the heart of the strike, and a United States mint was established there. Before it was established, the U.S. mint in Philadelphia by the end of 1832 had received more than half a million dollars' worth of gold deposits from the Cherokee Nation goldfields. The Cherokees received no compensation for the loss of these minerals from their lands.

When the gold rush began, the Cherokees appealed to their federal agent for help, who ordered United States troops into the goldfields. The troops attempted to evict the gold miners, which proved to be a nearly impossible task. Whenever the troops left one area for another, miners flooded back in behind the troops. The federal action angered the governor of Georgia, who appealed to President Andrew Jackson to remove the troops. Jackson, who had just gotten the United States Congress to pass the Indian Removal Act of 1830, complied with the request, and Georgia formed a special militia called the Georgia Guard to police the goldfields.

Immediately after the discovery of gold, the Georgia legislature enacted a law on December 20, 1828, declaring that as of June 1, 1830, all laws and customs of the Cherokee Nation would become null and void and that Cherokees would then be subject to Georgia law. Another law, aimed at white missionaries in the Cherokee Nation who were supporting the Cherokees in their fight against removal, mandated that any white person in the Cherokee Nation must take an oath of allegiance to the state of Georgia. Two missionaries, Samuel A. Worcester and Dr. Elizur Butler, refused to take the oath and were convicted in state court and sentenced to four years at hard labor. They appealed their convictions to the United States Supreme Court and won, with the Supreme Court striking down Georgia's attempt to extend its laws to the Cherokee Nation. In this 1832 case, known as *Worcester v. Georgia*, Chief Justice John Marshall, writing the majority opinion of the court, said "The Cherokee Nation . . . is a distinct community, occupying its

An undated photo, probably taken in the U.S. Southwest, of a tavern called the Randsburg Saloon. The Randsburg was typical of the businesses that sprouted up in the western United States following the explosive influx of non-Native people in search of gold and other valuable minerals in the 1800s.

own territory . . . in which the laws of Georgia can have no right to enter but with the assent of the Cherokees. The Act of the state of Georgia . . . is consequently void."

However, the new governor of Georgia, Wilson Lumpkin, refused to abide by the ruling. The two missionaries remained in a Georgia prison, and the Georgia Guard continued to enforce Georgia law in the Cherokee Nation. John Ridge led a Cherokee delegation to Washington, D.C., where they were told by President Jackson that he had no intention of enforcing the Supreme Court decision. Jackson told the Cherokees to return home and prepare to be removed to the West, which they were shortly forced to do.

The experience of the Cherokees in the Southeast in confronting the greed for gold would soon be repeated in varying degrees by Native peoples throughout the continent, wherever gold was discovered. In California, aside from the immediate and drastic impact upon Native peoples in that region, the discovery of gold there in 1849 had con-

sequences for Native peoples far removed from the California goldfields. The California gold rush brought an immediate need for linking the East and West Coasts with mail and passenger services. This led to the construction of stagecoach lines that affected Native peoples all across the continent. Stage lines were followed by railroad lines, and within a generation of the discovery of gold in California, there was hardly any region of the continent that was not easily accessible to white immigration. In Indian Territory, now the eastern portion of the state of Oklahoma, Native peoples were soon overwhelmed by a flood of white immigration along the railroad lines that, by the 1870s, made Indian people a minority population within their own nations.

In some areas, the discovery of gold or silver led quickly to statehood. In what is now Nevada, gold prospectors found gold in the area in 1859, setting off a rush, and they soon stumbled upon the Comstock Lode near Virginia City, which became the world's most productive silver mine. In a very short time, the population of Nevada swelled, and by 1864, it had become a state. Colorado was a part of Kansas Territory in 1859 when gold was discovered in the mountains west of Denver. By 1876, it had become a state. It might be noted that one of the first settlements in the area, near Denver, was named Auraria, after the Georgia boomtown in the goldfields of the Cherokee Nation.

Gold or silver was discovered throughout a large expanse of the West. In southern New Mexico, rushes occurred at Piños Altos, Silver City, and Orogrande. There were strikes in Arizona at Tombstone, Chloride, Prescott, and Wickenburg; in Utah at Ophir; in Wyoming at South Pass; in Nevada at Virginia City, Rawhide, Tonopah, and Goldfield; in Idaho at Coeur D'Alene, Moscow, Florence, and Boise; in Colorado at Central City, Leadville, Cripple Creek, Telluride, and Creede; in Montana at Helena, Butte, Virginia City, and Bannack; in South Dakota in the Black Hills at Deadwood and Lead; in California throughout the Sierra Nevada range east of San Francisco Bay; and in Alaska in the Klondike and at Nome. Wherever gold and silver miners rushed, Native people soon found themselves overwhelmed by a lawless population that had no regard for their rights.

Today, Native peoples still find themselves suffering at the hands of the extraction industries. The materials sought are more likely to be uranium or coal, rather than gold or silver, and government manipulation of tribal governments and industry corruption of tribal leaders is more likely to be employed than force in achieving the goals of the extraction industries.

But rarely have Native peoples benefited from the exploitation of mineral resources on their lands, frequently finding themselves with contracts that offer less than adequate compensation and that leave their lands scarred and tarnished. Very few tribal governments have a freedom of information act, which makes it difficult for Native investigative journalists to discover when corrupt tribal officials are entering into contracts that benefit everyone except the Native people. The experience of Native peoples on this continent with the American mineral extraction industries started badly in the early eighteenth century, got worse as that century progressed, and continues to be a problem for Native peoples today.

— D. L. Birchfield

SEE ALSO:
Black Hills; Removal Act, Indian; *Worcester v. Georgia.*

SUGGESTED READINGS:
Beck, Warren A., and Ynez D. Haase. *Historical Atlas of the American West.* Norman: University of Oklahoma Press, 1989.
Forbes, Jack D. *Native Americans of California and Nevada.* Rev. ed. Happy Camp, CA: Naturegraph, 1989.
Rensi, Ray C., and David Williams. *Gold Fever: America's First Gold Rush.* Atlanta: Georgia Humanities Council, 1988.
Young, Otis E., Jr. "The Southern Gold Rush, 1828–1836." *The Journal of Southern History.* 47, no. 3 (1982), pages 373–392.

GOOSE, MARY (1955–)

Native writer Mary Goose was born July 17, 1955, in Des Moines, Iowa. Goose dates her interest in creative literature from the time she was a small child, when her mother read comics to her and translated them into the Mesquakie language. Until she was in the third grade, Goose lived at the Mesquakie settlement near Tama, Iowa. Though she is of both Mesquakie and Ojibwe (Chippewa) heritage, her primary Native influences have been from the Mesquakie, which is her mother's tribe.

After attending schools in both Des Moines and Tama, Iowa, Goose graduated from Tama High School in 1974. She earned a B.A. in anthropology in 1980 and a B.S. in speech communication in 1985 from Iowa State University. In 1983, her creative work appeared in two of the most important early anthologies of Native writing, *Songs from This Earth on Turtle's Back: Contemporary Native American Poetry* (Greenfield Review Press) and *The Clouds Threw This Light* (Navajo Community College Press). Also in 1983, her poetry appeared in *North Dakota Quarterly.*

Since then, her work has appeared internationally, in *Estuaires, Revue Culturelle* (Luxembourg). She has developed an interest in writing and producing films and has reported on such events as the Native American Film Festival in Scottsdale, Arizona, for *News from Indian Country* and has become editor of the *Native American Producers Alliance Newsletter*. In 1992, she participated along with nearly four hundred Native writers in the Returning the Gift conference at the University of Oklahoma, and in 1994 her creative work appeared in the anthology that resulted from that conference, *Returning the Gift: Poetry and Prose from the First North American Native Writers' Festival* (University of Arizona Press). She has had a lifelong interest in science fiction and hopes to work in film in that genre.

SEE ALSO:
Returning the Gift.

GORDON, ROXY (1945–)

Choctaw playwright, poet, and performing artist Roxy Gordon was born March 7, 1945, in Ballinger, Texas. A prolific writer, he has published more than two hundred poems, articles, and stories in such publications as *Rolling Stone, Village Voice, Texas Observer, Greenfield Review, Dallas Times-Herald,* and *Dallas Morning News.* Since 1992, his weekly column has appeared in the *Coleman Chronicle & Democratic Voice* in Texas.

His fiction has been anthologized in *Earth Power Coming,* edited by Simon J. Ortiz (Navajo Community College Press, 1983). His volumes of poetry include *Unfinished Business* (1985), *West Texas Midcentury* (1988), *Small Circles* (1990), and *Revolution in the Air* (1994), all published by Wowapi Press of Dallas, Texas. In 1991, Sunstrom Records of London, England, produced an audiocassette of his poetry, titled *Smaller Circles.* Two other record albums of Gordon's work have been produced.

Perhaps his best-known work is as a playwright in collaboration with Choctaw writer LeAnne Howe. Their first play, *Big Powwow,* was performed in Dallas. Another collaboration, *Indian Radio Days,* was performed live on public radio in Iowa City, Iowa, in 1994, with satellite uplinks to Canada and Alaska. At that performance, Howe was interviewed about their collaborative techniques for the *Native Playwrights Newsletter.*

Gordon is an active storyteller and performing artist. His recent appearances include the Cowboy Poetry Festival in Kerrville, Texas, and the Leonard Peltier Benefit in Taos, New Mexico. Though he is of Choctaw descent, Gordon has spent much time with the Assiniboines. In July of 1991, he was adopted into the Assiniboine tribe at the Fort Belknap Reservation in northern Montana. He was adopted by the John and Minerva Allen family in a traditional ceremony at the Assiniboine Sundance. His new name is Toe Ga Juke Juke Gan Hok Sheena, which means First Coyote Boy.

GORMAN, R. C. (1932–)

Navajo artist R. C. Gorman is one of the foremost contemporary Native American artists, having received numerous prestigious awards and honors. He is the only living artist to be included in the show "Masterworks from the Museum of the American Indian," at the Metropolitan Museum of Art in New York City in 1973.

Gorman was born in 1932 on the Navajo reservation at Chinle, Arizona, and is descended from traditionalists and artists on both sides of his family, the most notable being his father, Navajo artist Carl Nelson Gorman. It has been said that his artistic talents had evolved through generations of exceptional people in his family tree. Among those family members were sand painters, weavers and silversmiths, a long line of holy men, and the Navajo leader Manuelito.

R. C. Gorman was raised in a traditional Navajo way—living in a hogan and herding sheep with his grandmother. His early influences are reflected in the designs and images of his artwork, many of which honor Navajo women. Depicted in his most famous artwork are Navajo women going about daily life—picking corn, nursing babies, building fires, or simply sitting in various poses wrapped in colorful blankets. His art evokes images that proclaim such things in life as timelessness and gracefulness.

R. C. Gorman studied art at the Northern Arizona University, later receiving a grant from the Navajo Tribal Council to study art at Mexico City College. His art has been a great influence and inspiration for people around the world.

Navajo artist R. C. Gorman is from a family with a rich tradition of artistic talent. Here, Gorman is at work in his home in Taos, New Mexico.

GOULD, JANICE (1949–)

Native writer Janice Gould, of Konkow and Maidu heritage, was born April 1, 1949, in San Diego, California. She moved to Berkeley, California, when she was nine years old, and she graduated from high school there in 1967. In 1983, she received a B.A. in linguistics, and in 1987 an M.A. in English, from the University of California at Berkeley. She is presently completing a Ph.D. in English at the University of New Mexico. In addition to being a writer, Gould is also a musician, preferring folk music. She plays the oboe, guitar, mandolin, and accordion. Her mother was trained in classical music at the Juliard School of Music in New York.

Gould's poetry has appeared in many publications, among them *Sinister Wisdom, Calyx: A Journal of Art and Literature by Women, Ikon, Berkeley Poetry Review, Conceptions Southwest, Evergreen Chronicles, Callaloo,* and *Fireweed.* She published an essay in the January 1994 Native American special issue of *Ariel: An International Journal of Literature in English* at the University of Calgary. Her work has been widely anthologized in such collections as *A Gathering of Spirit: A Collection by North American Indian Women* (Firebrand Books, 1984), *Living the Spirit: A Gay American Indian Anthology* (Stonewall Inn Press, 1988), *The Colour of Resistance: A Contemporary Collection of Writing by Aboriginal Women* (Sister Vision Press, 1993). In 1992, she participated in the Returning the Gift festival of nearly four hundred Native writers at the University of Oklahoma and contributed poetry to its anthology, *Returning the Gift: Poetry and Prose from the First North American Native Writers' Festival* (University of Arizona Press, 1994). Her short story appeared under the pen name Misa Gallagher in *Spider Woman's Granddaughters: Traditional Tales and Contemporary Writing by Native American Women* (Beacon Press, 1989). She has creative work or essays in a number of collections, including *Reinventing the Enemy's Language; Decolonizing the Subject: Politics and Gender in Women's Autobiography: An Intimate Wilderness;* and *Growing Up Different.*

In 1988, Gould received a grant for poetry from the National Endowment for the Arts (NEA), and in 1993, she received a writing grant from the ASTRAEA Foundation. In 1990, she published her first book of poetry, *Beneath My Heart* (Firebrand Books).

Janice Gould is an accomplished writer of prose, poetry, and fiction.

SEE ALSO:
Returning the Gift.

GOURD DANCE

The gourd dance honors the warriors' role in Indian nations and is for the warriors' society. Originally, the warriors would dance upon coming home from a battle. This was a great time of celebration, a time when warriors could tell their stories and be honored for their bravery and courage. The dance nearly died out when warriors could no longer be warriors in the traditional sense after the late nineteenth century, as their defensive fights for their land and people were stopped by near annihilation of the tribes and their confinement on reservations.

But the dance was brought back in the early to mid-1900s when elders sang the gourd dance songs and remembered the meaning behind the songs. After World War I, the elders noticed something missing for the Indian soldiers of the United States— the warriors' societies and the dancing, storytelling, and honors that had once been bestowed upon them and the feeling of accomplishment that went with the societies. To counter that lack, the gourd dance was brought back into existence. And though the dance had originated among the Kiowas and was used by other Plains nations, the elders opened the dance to all tribes. However, the dancers themselves are chosen by the warriors' society before they are permitted to dance the gourd dance.

The gourd dance is usually the first dance at a powwow with the dancers wearing a blanket over the right shoulder and carrying a fan, a rattle, or gourd. This dance is a man's dance, with the men inside the dance arena. The women, who may be dancing for husbands or other male relatives, dance on the outside of the arena just inside the boundaries.

Gourd dancers' clothing has great significance, and dancers have been instructed to wear their finest clothing while gourd dancing. Dancers will wear a dress shirt, slacks, and boots and rarely a cap or hat. The blanket is worn in one of three different ways according to the tradition in which the dancer has been instructed. In "Grandfather's way," the blanket is draped over both shoulders and hangs down in front. The blanket may also be draped over the right shoulder, hanging down the left side, crossing over the hip; the dancer holds the material while holding a fan in his left hand. In the third tradition, the blanket can be draped around the hips; it's usually a white cloth or sheet and is tied and hangs down by the sash. The peyote blanket of the Native American Church has been adopted for this process.

The bandolier hangs from the left to the right and is traditionally made of Mescal beads; now nickel-plated beads are used. The sash fits on the right side and is made of cloth with two tassels at the bottom. The tassels are usually beaded, and the sash has fringe on the bottom. The bandolier and the sash are strictly ornamental. The fan must be held in the left hand but does not have to be made of eagle feathers; any kind of feathers are appropriate. The gourd, or rattle, is carried in recognition of the Native American Church and is to be held in the right hand. The peyote gourd will not be seen in the dance arena because the dance arena is not considered the appropriate place for it. However, aluminum shakers or rattles are used in the arena.

Traditional gourd dancers wear leggings with a black shawl in front, breastplates, silver armbands, the fan, and a gourd. They also wear a red apron and moccasins.

The starting song lets everyone know the dance is beginning, and nobody is to dance until the song has been sung at least four times. The dancers are signaled when the head singer hits the drum and the others join in, similar to a drumroll. The singers then start a steady beat, and the gourd dancers go into the arena. The songs, most of which are in the Kiowa language, progress with a faster tempo than the starting song. The minimum number of closing songs is four, but there are so many closing songs the singers may sing six or more before ending. The ending song is commonly known as "Charlie Brown." The Buffalo Dance is also a common ending.

With more and more Indian men joining the United States armed services and fighting in numerous wars (such as the conflicts in Korea, Vietnam, Grenada, and the Persian Gulf), the need for the gourd dance and warriors' societies is great. In it, the men returning from conflict are allowed recognition for their accomplishments as warriors.

— S. S. Davis

SEE ALSO:
Gourd Dance Society; Warriors.

GOURD DANCE SOCIETY

The Gourd Dance Society is a society of Indian male warriors that originated among the Kiowa people and other Plains nations. It is one of seven societies for warriors among the Plains Indian nations. Four of those societies no longer exist because, after being confined on reservations during the nineteenth and early twentieth centuries, warriors were no longer allowed to act as warriors. But traditionally, warriors had come back from expeditions and danced, told their stories, and were honored for their courage and bravery.

In the 1940s, elders were singing gourd dance songs, provoking tears in others who remembered the meaning of the songs. The elders decided the songs and the society should not vanish and revived the Gourd Dance Society to fit those Indian warriors who were involved in the United States armed forces or in conflicts with the United States. The gourd dance was then opened up to all tribal nations.

Members of the society choose who its members shall be. Usually a member is chosen because powwow and other dancers become familiar with each other over time after seeing each other often at the events. New gourd dancers are taught the meanings of the songs and regalia used in gourd dancing and the ways of the warriors' society. Some gourd dancers have not fought or are not veterans but are dancing for their fathers or other relatives. In this way, they are honoring their relatives' bravery and courage. To be accepted into the Gourd Dance Society is a great honor for today's warriors, and the society and dance are treated with dignity and respect.

SEE ALSO: Gourd Dance; Warriors.

GOVERNMENTS, NATIVE

Colonists arriving in eastern North America encountered variations of a Native American confederacy model of government, which occurred when nations joined together for their mutual benefit. These confederacies usually made decisions through consensus, with tribal members discussing an issue until most or all members agreed upon a course of action. This model was unfamiliar to the immigrants, who had been living in societies governed by queens, princes, and kings. The best known of these consensual governments was the Iroquois Confederacy, with whom the early colonists had much contact.

Although the consensus model of decision making seems to have been most often used across the continent, some Native peoples maintained societies that were strikingly different. For example, the Northwest Coast peoples paid great attention to political hierarchy and economic status within their communities.

However, all along the Atlantic seaboard, Indian nations had formed confederacies by the time they encountered European immigrants, from the Seminoles to the Cherokees and Choctaws. Other confederacies included the Iroquois and the Wyandots (Hurons), as well as the Penacook federation of New England. The Illinois Confederacy, the "Three Fires" of the Ojibwe (Chippewa), Ottawa, and Potawatomi, the Wapenaki Confederacy, the Powhatan Confederacies, and the three-part Miami also were members of confederations.

The Iroquois's system was the best known to the colonists, in large part because of their pivotal position in diplomacy not only between the English and French, but also among other Native confederacies. Called the Iroquois by the French and the Five (later Six) Nations by the English, the Haudenosaunee (the word is Iroquois for "People of the Longhouse") controlled the only relatively level land pass between the English colonies on the Atlantic seaboard and the French settlements in the Saint Lawrence Valley.

European and Euro-American politicians and philosophers from Benjamin Franklin to Frederick Engels expressed astonishment at how the Iroquois and other Native American groups kept their peoples together peacefully and resolved interpersonal conflict without lawyers, jails, and edicts. Instead of formal instruments of authority, such as judges, courts, and police officers, the Iroquois governed behavior by instilling a sense of pride and connectedness to the group through common rituals. Ostracism and shame were the punishments for wrongdoings until a person had atoned for his or her actions and demonstrated this atonement through a purification process.

This Iroquois delegation, in November 1994, is commemorating the two-hundredth year of a treaty between the Iroquois and the United States. More than five thousand people gathered to witness the commemoration.

The system of the Wyandots was remarkably similar to that of their neighbors, the Iroquois. According to Bruce J. Trigger's *Children of the Aataentsic: A History of the Huron People,* the Wyandots' political system, like the one used by the Iroquois, was rooted in family structure. Leaders of the various clans used public opinion and consensus to shape decisions. Issues "were usually decided upon by majority vote . . . [and] discussed until a general consensus was reached." No human being would be expected to be bound by a decision to which he or she had not given conscious consent.

As with the Iroquois, the Wyandot clans—Porcupine, Snake, Deer, Beaver, Hawk, Turtle, Bear, and Wolf—created an affinity that reached across the boundaries of the four confederated Wyandot nations. Members of each clan could trace their ancestry to a common origin through the female line. In each village, clan members elected a civil chief and a war chief. The titles were carried through the female family line but bestowed on men, again resembling the Iroquois. While the titles were hereditary in that sense, they did not pass from head to head of a particular family, as in most European monarchies. When time came to choose a leader, members of each clan segment in a particular village had a choice of several candidates, among whom, according to Trigger, personal qualities counted most heavily—"intelligence, oratorical ability, reputation for generosity and, above all, performance as a warrior."

The four Wyandot nations—the Attignawantan, Arendarhonon, Attigneenongahac, and Tahontaeanrat—held a central council, which, according to Trigger, probably consisted of all the village chiefs representing all the clans. The central council dealt with issues that affected all four nations, such as treaty negotiations and trade with Europeans.

The Cherokee people, who call themselves Ani-Yunwiya ("The Real People" or "The Principal People"), were organized in settlements scattered in fertile bottomlands among the craggy peaks of the Great Smoky Mountains. The Cherokees took public opinion so seriously that they usually split their villages when they became too

In the nineteenth century, the Choctaw Capitol Building was constructed near the center of the nation at Tuskahoma, near present-day Clayton, Oklahoma. Today, the building houses a tribal museum, and the Choctaw Tribal Council meets each month in a modern facility nearby.

large to permit each adult a voice in council. In the early eighteenth century, the Cherokee nation comprised sixty villages in five regions, with each village controlling its own affairs. The villages averaged three hundred to four hundred persons each; at about five hundred people, a village usually split in two. Villages sent delegates to a national council only in times of national emergency.

The Cheyennes maintained a powerful central government that united the various Cheyenne bands. At the head of this organization was the Council of Forty-Four, on which civil chiefs served ten-year terms. The Cheyenne system closely resembled the Sioux "Seven Fires" confederacy, although the Sioux were not as tightly organized.

Six Cheyenne military societies served as police as well as organizers of war parties. These voluntary organizations were open to all men in the nation and were similar to the police societies of the Lakotas. All of these societies grew out of the horse culture of the Plains. The military societies

often carried out the council's orders. As the periods of peace dwindled with the onset of the Euro-American invasion, the police societies evolved into war societies that took over much of the authority of the Council of Forty-Four.

Cheyenne oral tradition says that the Council of Forty-Four was started by a woman, but its members were male. New chiefs were chosen by the council itself to replace those who left it at the end of their terms. George Bird Grinnell's description of a Cheyenne chief's demeanor sounds remarkably similar to the behavior that was expected of Iroquois sachems under their Great Law of Peace:

A chief must be brave in war, generous in disposition, liberal in temper, deliberate in making up his mind, and of good judgement. A good chief gave his whole heart and his whole mind to the work of helping his people, and strives for their welfare with an earnestness and a devotion rarely equalled by other rulers of men. Such thought for his fellows was not without its influence on the man himself. After a time, the spirit of goodwill which animated him became reflected in his countenance, so that, as he grew old, such a chief came to have a most benevolent and kindly expression. Yet, though simple, honest, generous, tender-hearted, and often merry and jolly, when occasion demanded, he could be stern, severe, and inflexible of purpose. Such men, once known, commanded general respect and admiration.

The peoples who occupied the West Coast of North America from the Alaska panhandle to the extreme northwest coast of Washington State departed from the general reliance on a consensus model of government. This departure was not slight. Their system was entirely different: status driven, caste bound, and, compared to many Native peoples, very aggressive, even among peoples who shared cultures very similar to their own. From the Chickliset in the north to the Makah in the south, the Northwest Coast peoples took sturdy whaling canoes to sea. In times of war, which occurred with a frequency and intensity that usually surpassed most peoples in North America, the canoes could be used for raiding and to capture slaves from neighboring Native nations.

Northwest Coast peoples generally recognized three social classes that seemed as imperishable as the red cedar from which they constructed their lodges: nobility, commoners, and slaves. The nobility was comprised of chiefs and their closest relatives; the eldest son was the family head. He, his family, and a few associates lived in the rear right-hand corner of the house, next to people of lower status. These people were said to be "under the arm" of the chief.

The next highest ranking chief, usually a younger brother of the head chief, invariably occupied the rear left-hand corner of the house, with his family. He, too, had a number of people "under the arm." The other two corners were occupied by lesser chiefs' families.

The space between the corners along the walls was used by commoners' families, and a few very junior-ranking nobility. They were called "tenants," while the nobility in the corners reserved the right to ownership of the house. Commoners could move from one house to another at will, and since they often performed arduous but necessary skilled labor (such as carpentry or whaling), chiefs competed to retain the best workers. The most successful chiefs were affectionate and generous toward the common families who chose to live in their lodges. Slaves had no designated lodgings or rights; they were captured in raids of other peoples along the coast and sometimes traded for other slaves, or goods. A noble in one village could be captured and sold into slavery in another. The captive's relatives might then mount a counterraid to free him.

It is evident that many different forms of government had evolved on the continent by the time of the arrival of Europeans. Numerous other forms could be cited, which might include the powerful roles of religious leaders in the traditional form of government of Isleta Pueblo in the Southwest and the last remnant of Temple Mound culture among the Natchez in the lower Mississippi River Valley. But the consensus forms of government of the eastern confederacies had the greatest influence on the colonists, and many of those influences would eventually be seen in the form of government adopted by the United States.

— B. E. Johansen

SEE ALSO:

Consensus in Native American Governance; Deganawidah; Hiawatha; Iroquois Confederacy; Isleta Pueblo.

SUGGESTED READINGS:

Bowers, Alfred W. *Mandan Social and Ceremonial Organization*. Chicago: The University of Chicago Press, 1950.

Drucker, Philip, *The Northern and Central Nootkan Tribes*. Bureau of American Ethnology Bulletin No. 144. Washington, D.C.: Smithsonian Institution, 1951.

Grinnell, George Bird. *The Cheyenne Indians: Their History and Ways of Life* [1923]. New York: Cooper Square Publishers, 1962.

Reid, John Phillip. *A Better Kind of Hatchet: Law, Trade and Diplomacy in the Cherokee Nation During the Early Years of European Contact*. University Park: The Pennsylvania State University Press, 1976.

Trigger, Bruce G. *Children of the Aataentsic: A History of the Huron People*. Montreal: McGill-Queen's University Press, 1976.

GRADUAL CIVILIZATION ACT

The purpose of the Gradual Civilization Act of Canada (passed in 1857) was to assimilate Canada's population of indigenous peoples into the larger non-Indian society. Although the British Crown had originally assumed responsibility for Native peoples, by the mid-nineteenth century, French and English colonists had made Canada their homeland and established a form of government. While warring colonial powers had once sought the allegiance of their Native allies, that role had changed as the number and size of settlements increased; the Indians were then seen as an obstacle to Canada's further growth as a nation. Colonists believed that if the Indians became citizens and swore allegiance to the crown, they would eventually merge with white society and Native cultures would eventually become extinct.

Although Indians inhabited the area now known as Canada long before the Europeans' arrival, the colonists did not recognize them as citizens. Missionaries believed that if the Indians were educated in the European way and were taught European farming methods, they could function within the new society. The Gradual Civilization Act stipulated that, to become citizens, Indians had to meet these new standards before an appointed board. To qualify, individuals had to be debt-free and of good moral character, and have a certain level of education. If individuals met these standards, they were given the rights of citizenship and almost fifty acres (twenty hectares) of land.

But historically, the Indian land base was communal. To divide land into individual plots went against tribal integrity and belief systems. Thus, the act clearly meant to detribalize Indians and disrupt the core of their cultures. The act also defied the British Royal Proclamation of 1763, which recognized Indian peoples as citizens of separate nations within the country. By offering citizenship, the Gradual Civilization Act implicitly defined Indians as noncitizens in their original status. This also affected negotiations over land that had been under the jurisdiction of the Proclamation of 1763.

The Gradual Civilization Act failed in its attempt to assimilate Indians. Only one individual met the requirements and actually was considered for citizenship. Not until 1860 did Britain transfer responsibilities for Indian matters to the British North American colonies, giving the colonists the right to attempt other assimilation through legislation, a process that was to continue in modified forms to the present day.

GRANT, ULYSSES S. (1822–1885)

Commander of United States forces late in the Civil War and eighteenth president of the United States (1869–1877), Ulysses S. Grant tapped Colonel Ely Parker, a Seneca, to become the first Native American commissioner of the Bureau of Indian Affairs. Parker had been secretary to Grant during the Civil War and wrote the surrender that General Robert E. Lee signed at Appomattox, formally marking the end of the Civil War.

Grant asked Parker to head the Indian Bureau as investigations of its operations by Congress under Senator James B. Doolittle found corruption. These findings were one part of a wave of scandals that plagued Grant, who was inexperienced in politics and, at age forty-six, the youngest person to be elected president of the United States to that time. The Doolittle report received considerable publicity; it found, "In a large number of cases, Indian wars are to be traced to the aggressions of lawless white men, always to be found upon the frontier." Parker came into office under the auspices of the Peace Policy initiated by Congress after the publicity attending the Doolittle report.

Grant's plans to reform the BIA were doomed as Parker was driven from office by the corrupt "Indian rings" that had profited so handsomely from government contracts for services paid but rarely delivered. During Parker's tenure as Indian commissioner, however, he helped orchestrate considerable public outrage over the treatment of Indians nationwide, particularly those on the Plains who were being ruthlessly pursued while he served in the office.

Grant and Parker had overseen a brief interlude in the destructive Indian policies of the nineteenth century, a time during which Red Cloud and his allies had forced the U.S. Army to dissemble its forts in the Powder River country and sign the Treaty of 1868, guaranteeing the Black Hills to the

During the presidency of Ulysses S. Grant (shown on the left in his days with the Union Army), the government stopped entering into treaties with Indian nations and proclaimed that Indian people were subject to the will of Congress.

Lakotas. In 1871, Grant appointed a review board to oversee the BIA. He also advocated replacing civilian Indian agents, whose interest was usually profit, with agents referred by churches. The era of treaty making was also ended by Congress during the Grant administration, in 1871, and Indians became subject to the will of Congress. Despite the scandals, Grant won reelection easily in 1872 over Horace Greeley.

See also:
Bureau of Indian Affairs; Parker, Ely; Red Cloud.

GRASS DANCE

See Dance, American Indian.

GREEN CORN CEREMONY

In terms of religious life, the highlight of Southeastern tribes, such as the Creeks, Seminoles, Cherokees, Choctaws, and Chickasaws, has traditionally been the Green Corn ceremony that must be observed before the new corn crop can be eaten. Taking place in late July or early August, Green Corn is a time of renewal, the beginning of the new year, when individuals and communities are ritualistically purified and focused on living in right relationship with earth and kin. Dances and ceremonies are performed for this purpose.

A skillful description of the Green Corn ceremony is contained in Willie Lena's book, *Oklahoma Seminoles: Medicine, Magic, and Religion* (University of Oklahoma Press), written with anthropologist James H. Howard. Green Corn lasts three days, starting on a Thursday and ending on Sunday, though many families camp all week to get things ready by Thursday. Activities include special dances like the Ribbon Dance, the Feather Dance, and the Buffalo Dance; nighttime stomp dancing around the sacred fire that is ritualistically rekindled during Green Corn; fasting and the taking of medicine by men and women; and assigning names to new members of the ceremonial grounds. Oklahoma Creeks and Seminoles still have around eighteen active ceremonial grounds, and Cherokees have active grounds as well.

A Cochiti Green Corn Dance, as depicted in 1947 by Joe Hilario Herrera.

GREEN, RAYNA (1942–)

Cherokee writer Rayna Green is a prolific poet, essayist, scholar, short story writer, and editor. She was born July 18, 1942, in Dallas, Texas, but was raised in Oklahoma. She received a B.A. (1963) and M.A. (1966) from Southern Methodist University. In 1973, she received a Ph.D. in folklore and American studies from Indiana University. A college teacher for much of her career, she has taught at Dartmouth College, Yale University, the University of Arkansas, the University of Massachusetts, the University of Maryland, and George Washington University. Presently, she is director of the American Indian Program at the National Museum of American History at the Smithsonian Institution in Washington, D.C.

Green's poetry has appeared in *Greenfield Review*, *Corona*, *Frontiers*, *American Indian Literature*, and *Massachusetts Review* and has been anthologized in *Durable Breath: Contemporary Native American Poetry* (Salmon Run Press, 1994). She is the author of more than forty scholarly essays, articles, and reviews, which have appeared in a wide variety of publications, including *Ms. Magazine*, *American Art Magazine*, *Folklore*, *Folklore Forum*, *Southern Exposure*, *Southern Folklore Quarterly*, and *The Digest*, and in anthologies, including *Temperature: A Centennial Retrospective* (Washington American Folklore Society, 1989), *Feminist Theory and the Study of Folklore* (University of Illinois Press, 1995), *Basketmakers: Meaning and Form in Native American Baskets* (Pitt-Rivers Museum, 1992), and *Aniyunwiya/Real Human Beings: An Anthology of Contemporary Cherokee Prose* (Greenfield Review Press, 1994). Her short fiction has been anthologized in *Talking Leaves: Contemporary Native American Short Stories* (Laurel, 1991).

She has edited two anthologies, *Pissing in the Snow and Other Ozark Folktales* (University of Illinois Press, 1977) and *That's What She Said: Contemporary Fiction and Poetry by Native American*

Rayna Green, director of the American Indian Program at the National Museum of American History.

Writers (Indiana University Press, 1984), and she has written two books, *Women in American Indian Society* (Chelsea House, 1991), and *Native American Women: A Contextual Bibliography* (Indiana University Press, 1984). She is also a writer of film and television scripts, including *More Than Bows and Arrows*, a sixty-minute color film produced by Cinema Associates in 1977. Another script, for *We Are Here: Pueblo Resistance for Five Hundred Years*, produced by the Smithsonian Institution, won the 1992 Cine Golden Eagle Award.

Green has also served as director of the Project on Native Americans in Science at the American Association for the Advancement of Science and was director of the Native American Science Resource Center at Dartmouth College. She has served on a number of boards, including the Phelps-Stokes Fund, the Indian Law Resource Center, and Ms. Foundation for Women.

GREENE, GRAHAM (1953–)

In the 1990s, Oneida actor Graham Greene seems to be an almost omnipresent representation of the American Indian. On TV, he has been the Navajo lawyer in *L.A. Law* and the Indian medicine man on *Northern Exposure;* on the movie screen, he has portrayed the militant Indian fighting to preserve the forest in *Clearcut,* the Indian policeman in *Thunderheart,* and the Sioux medicine man in *Dances with Wolves.* For his role as Kicking Bird in *Dances with Wolves,* he became the first Indian actor since Chief Dan George to be nominated for an Oscar.

But Greene's path to acting fame was not an easy one. Greene was born in 1953 on the Six Nations reserve near Brantford, Ontario. He was the second of six children born to John and Lillian Greene. Although he was raised on the reservation, his family was not traditional, and he was taught no Indian language nor any tribal traditions. His father worked as an ambulance driver and as a maintenance man. Greene has described his childhood as being very pleasant. At the age of sixteen, however, Greene struck out on his own. He dropped out of school and moved to Rochester, New York, where he got a job in a carpet warehouse. At eighteen, he returned to school at George Brown College and studied welding. After completing his training, he got a job in Hamilton, Ontario, building railway cars. In the early 1970s, he worked in the music industry as a roadie and soundman, and he ran a small music studio.

In 1974, he was asked to join a small Toronto theatrical group, and he played his first role, depicting an Indian. For the next few years, he played many small roles. In 1982, he teamed with other Indian actors in the play *Jessica,* which was about Indian assimilation. That same year, he gained his first movie role, playing the friend of Indian track star Billy Mills in the movie *Running Brave.* His next movie role was in *Revolution,* a 1984 movie about the American Revolution.

Greene's father died that same year, and his death seriously affected Graham. He entered into what he called his "warrior phase," a period filled with fast cars, guns, and camouflage suits. In the late 1980s, he had a few small acting roles and finally was reduced to selling T-shirts on the streets.

Greene's "big break" came when he was selected to play the part of one of the major Indian characters in director and actor Kevin Costner's *Dances with Wolves.* Costner originally rejected Greene for the role because with short hair, he did not seem "Indian enough." Now Greene's many rolls are having a positive effect in illustrating the many sides of contemporary North American Indian existence.

SEE ALSO:
Entertainment and the Performing Arts.

GREENLAND (KALAALLIT NUNAAT), INDIGENOUS PEOPLES OF

Known to the non-Inuit world as Greenland ever since Eric the Red misnamed it in 986 C.E., Kalaallit Nunaat is the largest noncontinent island on the planet and home to half of the Inuit people alive today. Over 1,500 miles (2,400 kilometers) long and 750 miles (1,200 kilometers) across, Greenland is slightly larger than Mexico. Yet precisely because it is *not* very green, and it *is* very cold, and because its resources have shown themselves to be too costly to mine for easy profits, the Inuit people of this land have survived with less hostility from Europeans than most other North American Native peoples. Nevertheless, attempted conquests or incursions over the past thousand years by Vikings, Danes, Christian missionaries, and North American tourists have threatened the Greenlandic Inuit and their way of life. Through it all, they have maintained many of their traditions while evolving and adapting to changing conditions.

Inuit people first came to Greenland from northern Canada about five thousand years ago, and for the next four thousand years, they lived challenged only by the Arctic climate. Although parts of the island are quite temperate and enjoy nearly twenty-four hours of daylight during the summer months, most of Greenland is ice-packed and besieged by intense winter storms for most of the year. Until recently, Inuit life on Greenland was sustained by fishing, hunting, and an ingenious ability to fashion tools, clothing, and shelter from the

A fisherman unloading his catch of fish at a harbor in West Greenland.

skin and bones of seals, polar bears, and other scant raw materials. They even used frozen fish to make dogsleds.

For thousands of years, the people lived a life patterned by the cycle of the year. Each winter, communities would gather in large stone or sod houses. They would share stored reserves of fish and meat, form large harpooning parties to increase their chances of success, and pass much of the winter by decorating tools and weapons, making boots and clothing, and reciting long, memorized narratives.

But each spring, the communities would break up into small, family-based hunting and fishing parties. Some traveled in kayaks and other small, skin-covered boats to fish and hunt seals. Others went north by dogsled, living in temporary igloos, to hunt larger land animals such as caribou. With the approach of winter, families would regather in their coastal communities, to honor in simple ceremonies the spirits and souls of animals and the landscape and to continue the cycle.

This way of life continued with little change for centuries. And although much of it is still practiced today, contact with outsiders is changing Native life in Greenland as much as the land and climate shaped it in the first place.

The first contact with outsiders came with the landmark journey of Eric the Red. Eric founded a small colony of Norwegian Vikings that his son, Leif Ericson, used as a base for his now-famous journeys to the North American mainland. The Vikings traded with the Inuits, whom they called the "Skraelings," but their settlement never flourished, and all traces of Viking life on Greenland seem to have vanished around the year 1400. Explanations for their mysterious disappearance vary from starvation to hostile attacks by Inuits to attack by English pirates.

The next contact by Europeans, 300 years later, has turned out to be far more consequential. Danish missionaries arrived in 1721 to establish the first in a series of settlements, and for the next 350 years the history of Greenland would be shaped by squab-

A Polar Inuit family at Moriussaq, in northern Greenland. A father holds his son, while the mother softens a kamik sole.

These children in Greenland are playing a game to welcome the sun.

bling and skirmishing among powerful world governments with no regard for the Inuit people. The missionaries brought Christianity to challenge the Inuit beliefs of animal spiritism and reincarnation. But the Danes brought smallpox, measles, tuberculosis, and influenza. Thousands of Inuit soon died from these unwelcome imports.

Throughout the nineteenth and early twentieth centuries, Norway and Denmark waged an ongoing, low-grade dispute over the "rights" to Greenland. The U.S. government got involved in 1917 when Denmark sold the Virgin Islands to the U.S. in exchange, in part, for U.S. recognition of Danish claims to Greenland. Neither the Native peoples of the Virgin Islands nor the Inuit of Greenland had anything to say about this, and in 1921, Denmark served Norway and the rest of the world notice of its sovereignty over Greenland.

When Germany invaded Denmark in World War II, the United States used the opportunity to establish a military presence on Greenland. The United States still maintains some weather, radar, and military operations there. After the war, Denmark changed Greenland's status from that of a ter-

ritory to part of the Danish kingdom, with two representatives in the *Folketing*, or Danish parliament.

Each contact introduced change for the Greenlandic Inuits, change over which they had no say, initiated by outsiders who never asked their permission. But in 1977, the Greenlandic Inuits participated in a historic conference with delegates from Inuit communities of Canada and Alaska. Seeking to take charge of their own economic and political destiny, Inuits declared their rights to self-government. Two years later, Denmark granted Greenland complete home rule, and plans were drawn up for a national Inuit homeland. Under this plan, the eastern half of Canada's Northwest Territories, a tract of over 750,000 square miles (1.9 million square kilometers), will pass into Inuit control by the year 2000. It will be called Nunavut, meaning "our land," but it remains to be seen whether—and how many—Greenlandic Inuits will be willing to leave their homeland of five thousand years.

Today, despite the accumulated effects of all the outside contacts and changes that continue to take place, the dominant characteristic of life in Greenland remains more Inuit than European. For all its landmass, Greenland has fewer than seventy-five thousand inhabitants. A few scattered communities in the north are entirely Inuit who live much as their ancestors did thousands of years ago. But the vast majority of Greenlanders are of mixed Inuit-European lineage, and they live in about seventy settlements, mostly along the western seaboard. The largest city, with a population of fifteen thousand, is the capital, Nuuk. Many maps will show Nuuk as Godthab, the Danish name for the city.

Though Inuit dialects are still spoken in the northernmost villages, people are more likely to speak Greenlandic, a hybrid of the most common Inuit dialects forged through an official effort in the mid-nineteenth century, and Danish. English is also widely spoken, a result of the United States military presence and recent North American tourism.

Tradition and change coexist everywhere. Fishing and hunting are still important, and many Inuit grow vegetables during the short, sunny summers, while others earn a living herding livestock, mining, working construction, and working as shopkeepers, merchants, publishers, and tour guides.

Traditional settlements continue to exist, but they now have schools, and each year Inuit schoolchildren judge an international Santa Claus competition, with "Santas" from countries all over the world parading their Yuletide talents before the children. There are still remarkably few paved roads, and igloos still dot the landscape. But snowmobiles scooting across the frozen fjords are an increasingly common sight, and all the settlements are linked by a state-of-the-art telecommunications network.

Ironically, the very inaccessibility that protected Native culture in Greenland through the centuries is now an attraction for the latest wave of outsider contact, ecotourism. Travel and tour agencies provide guides and plastic igloos complete with beds and plumbing for tourists who are eager to visit Inuit villages to observe, snap photos, and buy handicrafts from villagers.

— D. Press

SEE ALSO:
Alaska Natives; Inuit; Northwest Territories.

GROS VENTRES

The name *Gros Ventres*, pronounced "Groh VAN-truh," is French for "big bellies." The term was used by mistake to refer to two very different Indian tribes, the Algonquian-speaking Atsinas and the Siouan-speaking Hidatsas. Early French traders confused the two tribes and thought of them as one people because the hand gesture used in Indian sign language for the two tribes was nearly identical.

The Atsinas were once an Eastern Woodlands tribe, but in the early 1700s, they migrated to the Great Plains between the Saskatchewan and Missouri Rivers and roamed from Missouri to Canada. Mounted on horses, they followed the bison herds and lived by hunting. The Atsinas were related to the Arapahos, but the two tribes split soon after arriving on the Plains. There, the Atsinas were influenced by the ceremonial practices of the Hidatsas and began practicing the Sun Dance ceremony. During the 1700s, the Atsinas were allies of the Blackfeet.

The Hidatsas lived in earth lodges along the Missouri River in present-day North Dakota. They were a farming people and also made pottery. Part of the Hidatsa tribe left the Missouri River towns and moved to the Powder and Big Horn River area, where they became bison hunters, like the Atsinas. They called themselves *Absaroke*, which means "Crow-people." Over time, they were simply called "Crows."

Most of the Missouri River Hidatsas died from smallpox epidemics, and in 1781, smallpox struck the Atsinas. The tribe was further reduced by warfare with the Assiniboine, Cree, and Crow tribes. Before smallpox hit, the tribe numbered over 1,200, according to reports by European traders. By 1904, the tribe numbered just 534.

The surviving Atsinas were placed on the Fort Belknap Reservation with their former enemies, the Assiniboines. In 1991, the Assiniboines and Atsinas had a combined population of 2,407. Today, the tribes operate one of the thirty-one colleges in the American Indian Higher Education Consortium, Fort Belknap Community College, at Harlem, Montana.

SEE ALSO:
Assiniboine; Hidatsa.

GUADALUPE HIDALGO, TREATY OF

The Treaty of Guadalupe Hidalgo, which ended the Mexican War, had a great impact on Indian tribes in the Southwest and in California. Nicholas P. Trist represented the United States government in the treaty negotiations, but not without controversy. He disregarded almost all of the instructions that were given to him, plus a recall order to return to Washington. In the treaty, which was signed on February 2, 1848, Mexico ceded Arizona, New Mexico, and Alta (upper) California and acknowledged the United States' claims to Texas, with the Rio Grande as the boundary between Mexico and Texas. The United States paid Mexico $15 million and ceased all U.S. claims against Mexico. Under the treaty, the United States recognized all former land grants, and Indians were supposed to maintain title to their lands through "immemorial use and occupancy" of the land affected by the treaty.

This map highlights portions of Mexico (now part of the U.S. Southwest) that were ceded to the United States by the Treaty of Guadalupe Hidalgo.

By the terms of the treaty, all persons within the ceded lands who had been citizens of Mexico automatically became citizens of the United States, unless they declared their desire to remain citizens of Mexico within a specified time. Since the Pueblo Indians of New Mexico had been considered citizens of Mexico by the Mexican government, the Pueblos lost their status as Indians by the treaty. (A U.S. Supreme Court decision in 1872 affirmed that the Pueblos had ceased being Indians and had become citizens of the United States by the Treaty of Guadalupe Hidalgo. That decision was later

A painting by M. R. Poore depicts a pack train leaving Taos Pueblo, New Mexico. The Treaty of Guadalupe Hidalgo, which in 1848 put an end to the war between Mexico and the United States, had at least one unwanted effect on Pueblos living in former Mexican territory in the U.S. Southwest: It stripped them of their status as Indians.

overturned by a Supreme Court ruling in 1917, at which time Pueblos were once again able to pursue their legal rights as Indians, but only after much of their land and their water rights had already been encroached upon.)

In 1850, a special congressional Enabling Act called for treaties with the California tribes. Eighteen treaties were signed that took away 90 million acres (36 million hectares) of Indian land. California tribes were allowed to maintain approximately 9 million acres (3.6 million hectares) of land in California, but much of this land was unusable desert land. Even these treaties were opposed by white Californians who argued that Indians should receive no land. The treaties were ratified by the U.S. Congress, but they were then "lost" for several years in government archives.

In 1853, all Indian land in California was assigned as public domain. A land commission was formed the same year to hear alternate claims, but all hearings were held in San Diego, hundreds of miles away from some of the tribes. The government did not inform the tribes that they could come before the commission with claims. As a result, all Indian lands in California were ruled forfeited, and all land was seized without compensation.

Through later appeals to the U.S. government, some Indian lands were regained, but troubles with the government did not end there. In the 1930s, most California tribes were asked to accept the Indian Reorganization Act. Also known as the Indian New Deal, this act halted the breaking up and selling, or allotment, of Indian lands and permitted the organization of tribal governments for such functions as managing tribal funds and communal property. However, the Indian Reorganization Act carried so many restrictions and conditions, and the history of government dealings with tribes had such a history of increasing rather than decreasing the amount of hardship for Native people, that many Indians were reluctant to support it. Even though the act was opposed by most tribal members, when Bureau of Indian Affairs officials counted the votes, they announced that the Reorganization Act had been accepted.

Starting in the 1950s, the California tribes began to bring suits against the U.S. government in an attempt to gain redress for lands seized illegally and in violation of the Treaty of Guadalupe Hidalgo.

Indian tribes were required to use BIA-approved lawyers, and most claims by Indian tribes were rejected. As a final blow, in cases where Indian claims were upheld, damages were paid based on land prices from the 1830s, and the tribes received only 47.5 cents for each acre (0.4 hectare) of land.

— T. Colonnese

SEE ALSO:

General Allotment Act; Indian New Deal (Indian Reorganization Act); Mexican–American War.

GULLIVER'S TRAVELS AS PORTRAYAL OF AMERICA

In Jonathan Swift's *Gulliver's Travels*, American Indians may be represented by the Houyhnhnms, Swift's supremely rational horses, whose name in their own language was said by the author to mean "The Perfection of Nature." Swift, in the person of Gulliver, is called on to describe English society to the Houyhnhnms, who cannot comprehend the cruelties and follies of "civilized" life among Englishmen. "My master," he writes, referring to the horse to which he "belonged," "was yet wholly at a loss to understand what motives could incite this race of lawyers to perplex, disquiet, and weary themselves by engaging in a confederacy of injustice." English novelists later put similar words into the mouths of American Indian leaders such as Canassatego.

Likewise, the Houyhnhnms are at a loss to understand Europe's economy where, as Gulliver explains it, "the rich man enjoyed the fruits of the poor man's labor . . . that the bulk of our people are forced to live miserably, by labouring every day for small wages to make a few live plentifully." The Houyhnhnms could not reconcile such a system with their own, far more just system, which "went upon the supposition that all animals had a title to their share of the productions of the earth."

The original title of *Gulliver's Travels* was *Travels into Several Remote Nations of the World*. Swift's book, while purposefully fanciful and satirical, falls squarely within the type of travel literature that did so much to open Europe's eyes to the wonders of other continents during the Age of Discovery. Swift wrote his book as European explorers were sending home descriptions of traditional societies from Africa, Australia, and Asia, as well as the Americas. The Houyhnhnms could be a composite of Tasmanians, Africans, Aztecs, and Mohawks, more or less, all or none.

SEE ALSO:

Canassatego; European Attitudes Toward Indigenous Peoples; Noble Savage.

GUNS

Native Americans were introduced to guns by the arriving Europeans. Although the gun was of great advantage to Europeans in early fighting with Native American tribes, its value as a weapon was limited by the primitive nature of early firearms as well as by the tactical circumstances of their use. Though guns had a strong psychological impact on Native Americans at first, their mystique faded rapidly. In general, the bow and arrow were probably at least as effective as early guns, and not until the mid-1800s did the gun become a substantially more effective weapon than traditional Indian weapons.

Europeans carried matchlock and flintlock muzzleloaders up to the early 1800s. Matchlock guns employed a piece of smoldering cord called a "match" to ignite the propellant charge that would drive the bullet. Flintlocks used a piece of flint to create sparks for the same purpose. Virtually all of these guns were muzzleloaders that used black powder as a propellant.

To fire a muzzleloader, the shooter had to go through a complicated procedure that included the following steps: measuring and pouring in the powder; compressing the powder; forcing in the bullet and ramming it down the barrel; priming the gun; cocking the lock; aiming and firing. Even in the hands of an expert, a muzzleloader could

An illustration from *Gulliver's Travels* by Jonathan Swift shows Gulliver in the land of the Houyhnhnms, a race of sensible horses. The Houyhnhnms' reaction to the follies of so-called civilized European society may have been drawn from various traditional societies throughout the world, including Native America.

only be fired once for every six or so arrows fired from a bow.

Guns like the Kentucky rifle of this period had substantially greater range and power than bows. However, the tactical situation did not require such qualities. Through the early 1800s, most conflict took place in tree-covered swamps or forests, thus decreasing the maximum range at which one could sight a target. In addition, such areas were relatively damp; the shooter had to "keep your powder dry" or the gun wouldn't fire.

An Inuit hunter in northwest Greenland, armed with a high-powered rifle and scope. As rifles are replacing traditional hunting weapons, snowmobiles are also replacing dogsleds.

Mistakes in the complicated loading procedure could also keep these guns from firing, or even worse, cause injury to the shooter.

In the mid-1800s, a series of innovations such as percussion caps and metallic cartridges allowed guns to surpass the bow and arrow. Percussion caps are tiny explosive charges that are set off by a sharp blow from a gun's hammer. These caps are used in place of the match or flint to ignite the propellant powder. A metallic cartridge is a container, usually brass, filled with powder with a percussion cap at one end and a bullet at the other. Since a cartridge contains all the necessary ingredients expended in firing a gun, it greatly reduces the number of steps a shooter has to go through to reload. This speeds up reloading, making it simpler and less prone to dangerous mistakes. In addition, cartridges are almost impervious to water.

These innovations allowed the development of breech-loading and repeating guns. Breech-loading guns are ones in which the shooter manually opens the back of the barrel or "breech," inserts a cartridge, cocks the hammer, and fires the gun. In repeaters, several cartridges are stored in a part of the gun called a "magazine" and are fed mechanically into the breech. Breech-loading single-shot rifles like the Sharps of 1848 (from which the term *sharpshooter* is derived) could be fired about as quickly as a bow and were deadly accurate at several hundred yards (several hundred meters), much farther than the best bow. Repeaters like the Spencer and Henry, both of 1860, or the Winchester Lever-Action of 1866 were slightly less powerful than the Sharps but could be fired even more rapidly than a bow.

The effectiveness of these new guns was enhanced by the changing tactical situation. Settlers had spread to the Great Plains, and the majority of fighting between Native Americans and the United States government would be in this region. Lack of cover in the Plains increased the ranges at which shots could be taken. With their great range advantage on the Plains, guns were far more effective than any traditional Native American weapon. Properly employed, breech-loading guns were the decisive weapon in Plains fighting.

The importance of guns in Plains warfare has led to a number of interrelated myths and stereotypical characters. Hollywood westerns have perpetuated these in the often-told story of the "white outlaw" who sells guns to the Indians. These stories revolve around the notion that Native Americans had a hard time getting guns and had very few of them. In fact, guns were quite easy to get almost from the beginning.

To most European colonists, guns were essential tools that provided safety and food. These tools were obviously useful but could not be manufactured by the Native Americans at that time. This made them perfect trade goods. After the Revolutionary War, the U.S. government continued this trade through licensed and subsidized factories that sold or even gave guns to Indians. Guns were considered a "civilizing" influence, in part, because guns required ammunition. If the Native Americans could be made dependent on guns for hunting, then they would be dependent on the government for ammunition. Guns were provided sporadically under this policy through the early 1800s.

American Indians could gain the guns in a number of ways. European nations and the U.S. government gave guns to tribes they considered allies. Native American nations so armed provided bodies of troops in virtually every conflict in North America, and Indian troops often took these guns home after the war. A large number of guns were also given to Indian allies by both the Union and Confederacy during the U.S. Civil War. Even when a tribe was not an active ally, some of its members might volunteer to fight or act as scouts. These volunteers were often given guns. When a tribe was at war with the U.S. government, it could usually capture most of the guns and ammunition it needed. Overall, it was not too hard for the tribes of North America to arm themselves with guns when the need arose.

— L. Hester

SEE ALSO:
Weapons, Native American.

HAIDA

The Haidas are a people of the Northwest Coast whose territory encompasses the Queen Charlotte Islands in British Columbia. It is estimated that the Haidas, whose name means "the people," have lived on the islands for nine or ten thousand years.

For hundreds of years, the Haidas used the land and waters to make their living, but slowly, the lives

This photo of Haida people on Queen Charlotte Island, British Columbia, Canada, was taken in November 1953 after a church service.

of the Haidas began to change. Near the end of the eighteenth century, whites began to venture into the northern Pacific Ocean and the Queen Charlotte Islands. Traders came to obtain animal furs and skins. The Haidas traded animal skins with merchants from Spain, Britain, and Russia for manufactured goods such as knives, iron kettles, and needles. This contact brought many changes in Haida culture, as the Haidas adopted many aspects of Canadian and U.S. life. However, the Haidas have always been determined to maintain their traditional ways.

The Northwest Coast Indians are renowned for their woodcarving skills. Giant totem poles, boats, ceremonial masks, chests, and headdresses of the Northwest Indians are known throughout the world. The Haidas are perhaps the most skillful of woodcarvers, known for their elaborately carved and painted boats, enormous totem poles, and bark baskets.

The Haidas are also renowned for their cedar-planked houses, some of which were sixty to one hundred feet (eighteen to thirty meters). A Haida village stood along the beachfront, facing the sea; outside the houses, giant totem poles represented the family symbols of the residents of the house.

Traditionally, the Haidas' diet consisted of fish and marine mammals such as seals, sea lions, and sea otters. Shellfish was another staple, as well as deer, bear, plants, and berries. The lands and waters of the Haidas were rich with resources, and they enjoyed a diverse and nutritious diet.

The Haidas maintained a system of family ancestries that were linked into two large groups called Raven and Eagle. Members of the same clan were not allowed to marry, and children automatically belonged to the mother's group. Their communities were divided into three classes—the nobles, the commoners, and the slaves.

Haida potlatches were feasts hosted by the head of a family as a celebration or as occasions for competition among rival chiefs. A potlatch consisted of feasting and the giving away of valuables and goods. Great respect was owed to the chief who gave the most away. For many years, the government outlawed potlatches, as it did various expressions of Native culture. Nonetheless, the Haidas practiced potlatches in secret.

The Haidas have undergone a great many changes in the twentieth century with the influ-ence and presence of the missionaries and colonists. Today, there are two groups of Haidas called the Masset and the Skidegate, living in several different villages in British Columbia. Although the two bands are separate, they joined together in 1980 to form the Council of the Haida Nation. The Haidas of British Columbia and Alaska continue to value and practice many aspects of their traditional life and are committed to ensuring that it is passed on to future generations.

SEE ALSO:
Alaska; British Columbia; Giveaway.

HAIL, RAVEN (1921–)

Native writer Raven Hail, a member of the Cherokee Nation of Oklahoma, was born January 27, 1921, near Dewey, Oklahoma, in Washington County. She grew up on her mother's Cherokee allotment in Craig County near the town of Welch. Hail's close association with her Cherokee heritage during her early life can be seen in her public performances, where she uses both the English and Cherokee languages in her presentations, mixing the languages, with poetry and prose, in a way that engages her audiences. One of her books, titled *The Raven's Tales*, is a bilingual collection of Cherokee traditional stories.

Hail attended Oklahoma State University in Stillwater, Oklahoma, and Southern Methodist University in Dallas, Texas. She now makes her home in Arizona. Her recent public performances have included the Valle del Oro Theatre in Mesa, Arizona, creative writing workshops at Herberger Theatre in Phoenix, Arizona, and the Arizona Poetry Society in Mesa, Arizona.

Her poetry, essays, and stories have appeared in a wide variety of publications, ranging from newspapers to literary quarterlies to anthologies. These include *Fiction International, The Blue Cloud Quarterly, Indian Voice, Daybreak, The Cherokee Nation News, The Cherokee Advocate, Arizona Women's Voice, Poetry Dallas, Quetzaal, The Archer, Tosan, Gray Day, The Herbalist, The Herb Quarterly, Circle of Motion, Bestways Magazine, Nimrod, Cimarron Review, Translation, The Little Balkans*

Review, The State, Lacuna, Mr. Cogito, and *The Wayside Quarterly.* Her work was anthologized in two of the earliest and most important collections of Native American writing, *The Remembered Earth* and *The Clouds Threw This Light,* and it appears in one of the most recent collections, *Returning the Gift: Poetry and Prose from the First North American Native Writer's Festival.* At the Returning the Gift Festival, a conference of nearly four hundred Native writers at the University of Oklahoma in 1992, Hail was a presenter at a workshop on using history in creative writing.

From 1968 to 1972, Hail was editor of *The Raven Speaks,* a monthly journal of Cherokee culture. Her essays from the journal were later collected into a book by the same name. She is also the author of a three-act play, titled *The Raven and the Redbird,* about the life of Sam Houston and his Cherokee wife, Talihina Rogers. Hail has also published a coloring book for children titled *Native American Foods Coloring Book,* a novel titled *Windsong,* and a storybook titled *The Pleides Stones.*

Raven Hail, noted Cherokee storyteller, author, and editor.

HALE, JANET CAMPBELL (1947–)

Janet Campbell Hale is a well-known Native American author. Born in Riverside, California, she is a member of the Coeur d'Alene Nation of northern Idaho and is also part Kootenai on her mother's side. She attended the Institute of American Indian Arts in Santa Fe, New Mexico, from 1962 through 1964 and graduated from the University of California at Berkeley in 1974. She has taught at the University of California at Berkeley; the University of California at Davis; DQ University, which is a tribally owned and operated institution and a member of the American Indian Higher Education Consortium, in Davis, California; and at Northwest Indian College, near Bellingham, Washington, which is a tribal college, owned and operated by the Lummi Nation, and which is also a member of the American Indian Higher Education Con-

sortium. Hale has studied law at both the University of California at Berkeley and at Gonzaga Law School in Spokane, Washington. She is the author of four books—*Owl's Song* (1974), *Custer Lives in Humboldt County* (1977), *Jailing of Cecelia Capture* (1987), and *Bloodlines: Odyssey of a Native Daughter* (1993).

HALL, LOUIS (1918–)

Louis Hall, whose Mohawk name is Karoniaktajeh (meaning "Near the Sky"), is regarded as the ideological founder of the Warrior movement in Mohawk country. A Mohawk, he was a member of the Kahnawake reserve's traditional council in 1971 when it decided to approve of a group of young men who said they wanted to revive a warrior society there. As "keeper of the well," Hall took the young men's request under consideration and placed it on the council's agenda.

Unlike the Mohawk Nation Council at Akwesasne, the Longhouse at Kahnawake became advocates of the Warrior cause, so much so that in 1973, its members sought to have non-Indian families evicted from their reserve, a move opposed by the elective Band Council that Canada recognizes as the government of the reserve. Following that split at Kahnawake, a group of Mohawks inspired by Hall's beliefs started a settlement at Ganienkeh, New York, to carry out their nationalistic vision of Mohawk tradition, including farms, a sawmill, cigarette sales, and high-stakes bingo.

During 1990, the events in Mohawk Country were accompanied by a rising, often emotional, debate over the future of the Iroquois Confederacy as a whole. At the heart of this debate are two versions of history. One belongs to the Onondaga elders, the Mohawk Nation Council, and many of the other national councils that comprise the Iroquois's original political structure. These people reject violence and look at the Warriors as illegitimate usurpers of a thousand-year-old history. The other interpretation, supported by the Warriors and put together by Hall, rejects the governing structure as a creation of white-influenced religion (especially the Quakers) and advocates a revolution from within to overthrow it.

In 1990, as the Warriors captured headlines at Akwesasne, Kahnawake, and Kanesatake, Hall, then seventy-two years old, was living in a mobile home at Kahnawake. Hall's trailer was crammed with books surrounding the old Olympia typewriter on which he pounds out Warrior wisdom. He is a painter of stark images—many Warriors hang his works in their homes—and designer of the Warrior flag, as well as a Warrior recruiting poster modeled after the famous World War I image of Uncle Sam.

Hall's manifesto, "Rebuilding the Iroquois Confederacy," claims that the Warriors hold the true heritage of the Iroquois and that today's traditional council and chiefs at Akwesasne have sold out to elitism, the Quakers, Handsome Lake, and non-Indian interests in general. Hall regards the religion of Handsome Lake, which began as a series of visions in 1799, as a bastardized form of Christianity grafted onto Native traditions; he regards its followers, including many gambling opponents, as traitors or "Tontos." Louis Hall calls Handsome Lake's visions the hallucinations of a drunk. Opposition to these teachings is one plank in an intellectual platform that allows the Warriors to claim that the Mohawk Nation Council at Akwesasne, and the Iroquois Confederacy Council as well, are enemies of the people, and that the Warriors are the true protectors of "Mohawk sovereignty."

Leon Shenandoah, an Onondaga who is speaker of the Iroquois Confederacy, has been critical of Hall. Some opponents of Hall's ideology have also criticized his methods, warning that his appeals to nationalism can evoke emotions in the young that can lead them to irresponsible behavior.

—B. E. Johansen

SEE ALSO:

Akwesasne (St. Regis Reservation), Pollution of; Handsome Lake; Iroquois Confederacy; Mohawk.

HAMPTON INSTITUTE

The Hampton Normal and Agricultural Institute in Hampton, Virginia, was founded in 1868 to educate newly freed African-American slaves. It was also the forerunner of the federal boarding school system for Native Americans that was established in the late nineteenth century. The institute's founder, Samuel Chapman Armstrong, was born in Hawaii to missionary parents and educated at Williams College in Massachusetts. A leader of an African-American regiment during the Civil War, Armstrong's aim was "to train selected Negro youth who should go out and teach and lead their people, first by example . . . and in this way to build up an industrial system for the sake of character."

Hampton's involvement in American Indian education began in April 1878. The first group of Native American students, seventeen male former prisoners of war, arrived at Hampton from Fort Marion in St. Augustine, Florida. They were part of a larger group of tribal people imprisoned by the U. S. military in 1875 following the Red River War on the southern Plains. At the Fort Marion prison, the hostages were guarded by military officer Richard Henry Pratt, who eventually introduced a program of Euro-American instruction to them. These prisoners of war, primarily Cheyennes,

A variety of figures from American history at an Indian Citizenship Day pageant in 1892. One purpose of the pageant was to promote the assimilation of Native people into the dominant culture. The characters—all portrayed by Hampton Indian students—included pilgrims, Quakers, Pocahontas, Christopher Columbus, Captain John Smith, George Washington, and William Penn.

Kiowas, and Arapahos, also created artwork at Fort Marion, drawing scenes from their own cultures. This work, known as "ledger art," became famous for its artistry and for documenting tribal ways during a period of great upheaval for Native people.

At the end of three years in prison, the Fort Marion hostages were given the choice of returning home or remaining in the East for more schooling. Pratt, who wanted to extend the experiment in Euro-American education he had started, wrote to a number of schools to request that they admit some of the prisoners as students. Only Hampton's founder, Armstrong, agreed to try the experiment. Twenty-two of the former hostages remained in the East "to learn more of the white man's road." The majority were at Hampton, with the others in private placements. At the school, their schedule included work and study. Among the students was Koba (a Kiowa), who wrote of his schooling, "I pray every day and hoe onions."

A short time after the arrival of the Fort Marion students at Hampton, Armstrong and Pratt obtained support from the federal government to expand their experiment in Native education. Pratt, following the government's orders, traveled to Dakota Territory, in present-day North and South Dakota, to recruit more students. He returned to Hampton on November 5, 1878, with forty-nine students, forty males and nine females, from six tribal agencies.

These pioneering young people, the majority Sioux, joined the Fort Marion students, who helped them adjust to the difficult changes required at the school. By 1879, the government considered Hampton's program a success and established a federal Indian boarding school on a larger scale at military barracks in Carlisle, Pennsylvania. Pratt was placed in charge of the Carlisle Indian Industrial School, and most of Hampton's Fort Marion students followed him there.

Wearing tribal clothing obtained from the Hampton Institute's museum collection, a Sioux-Crow Creek student participates in a form of "show and tell" before an American history class made up of Native and African-American students in 1900. Classes often included lessons using objects relating to the Indians' past.

Hampton's historic American Indian program received federal support from 1878 to 1912 as a contract school. In 1912, however, the government ended its aid, largely because of controversy over educating Native Americans and African Americans together. Hampton Institute then continued the program on its own, with dwindling numbers of Native students, until 1923. During the Indian program's forty-five years of existence, over 1,300 students from sixty-five tribal groups attended the school. The largest tribe represented was Sioux (473 students), followed by Oneida (194), Seneca (112), Omaha (64), Winnebago (63), and Cherokee (61). Hampton's Native American alumni included James Bear's Heart (Cheyenne), a talented artist who remained at the school the longest of any of the Fort Marion students; George Bushotter (Lakota), who became known as "the first Lakota ethnographer"; Cracking Wing (Mandan), one of the Native students who died at the school and is buried in the campus cemetery; Angel De Cora Dietz (Winnebago), a gifted artist who served as the first instructor of Native American art at the Carlisle Indian school; William Jones (Sac and Fox), who earned a Ph.D. degree in ethnology; and Susan Picotte-LaFlesche (Omaha), who became the first female Native American physician in the country.

Hampton University, as the school is presently known, is a private institution of higher education. It offers bachelor's and master's degrees in a variety of fields as well as a Ph.D. in physics. Hampton University has an enrollment of approximately 5,700 students, the majority African American. The school's legacy in Native American education includes museum and archival collections documenting the historic Indian program as well as a scholarship program for present-day Native American students.

— P. Molin

SEE ALSO:
Bear's Heart, James; Boarding Schools; Bushotter, George; Carlisle Indian School; Dietz, Angel De Cora; Jones, William; Murie, James Rolfe; Picotte-LaFlesche, Susan.

HANCOCK, JOHN
(1736–1793)

In the midst of the debates over independence in the Continental Congress, twenty-one Iroquois Indians came to meet with the Continental Congress in May of 1776. The Indians lodged on the second floor of Independence Hall (then called the Pennsylvania State House), observing the debates at the invitation of the delegates.

On June 11, 1776, only three weeks before independence was declared, the visiting Iroquois chiefs were invited formally into the hall of the Continental Congress, where a ceremony was held. There, the colonists delivered a speech, calling the Iroquois chiefs "Brothers" and wishing that the "friendship . . . between us . . . will . . . continue as long as the sun shall shine . . ." and the ". . . waters run." The speech also declared that the colonists and the Iroquois be ". . . as one people, and have but one heart."

After this speech, an Onondaga chief asked to give John Hancock, who was president of the Continental Congress, an Indian name. The congress graciously consented, and the Onondaga chief gave the "president the name of *Karanduawn,* or the Great Tree."

SEE ALSO:
Declaration of Independence, U.S.; Iroquois Confederacy; Onondaga.

A portrait of John Hancock by painter John Singleton Copley.

HANDSOME LAKE (c. 1733–1815)

The religion of Handsome Lake, which began as a series of visions by a Seneca man in 1799, combined Quaker forms of Christianity with Native traditions. Its influence is still strongly felt among the traditional Iroquois, who often call the Code of Handsome Lake "The Longhouse Religion." Handsome Lake's personal name was Ganeodiyo;

"Handsome Lake," a reference to Lake Ontario, is one of the fifty chieftainship lines of the Iroquois confederacy. Handsome Lake was a half brother of the Seneca chief Cornplanter and an uncle of Red Jacket.

Handsome Lake was born at Conawagus, a Seneca village near contemporary Avon, New York, on the Genesee River. He and many other Senecas sided with the British in the French and Indian War and the American Revolution. After that war, many Iroquois and other Native Americans who had supported the British were forced into Canada or onto small impoverished reservations in the United States.

Handsome Lake's early life reflected the disintegration of his people. His birthplace was taken by whites, and Handsome Lake was forced to move to the Allegheny Seneca reservation. The Seneca ethnologist Arthur Parker characterized Handsome Lake as "a middle-sized man, slim and unhealthy looking . . . [who became] a dissolute person and a miserable victim of the drink."

After four years on his back in a small cabin, Handsome Lake began having a series of visions. With these visions, he later rallied the Iroquois—this at a time when some of them were selling their entire winter harvest of furs for hard liquor, turning traditional ceremonies into drunken brawls, and, in winter, often dying of exposure in drunken stupors. The Iroquois population in upstate New York had declined to roughly four thousand people by this time.

By the spring of 1799, Handsome Lake had experienced considerable remorse over his alcoholism, but didn't stop drinking until he was nearly dead. Parker wrote that Handsome Lake was "all yellow skin and dried bones."

Handsome Lake finally stopped his own heavy drinking and later included abstinence as part of his Code of Handsome Lake. He persuaded many other Iroquois to do the same. Handsome Lake achieved some political influence among the Senecas, but his popularity slid because of his ideological rigidity. In 1801 and 1802, Handsome Lake traveled to Washington, D.C., with a delegation of Senecas to meet with President Thomas Jefferson and to resist the reduction of their peoples' landholdings.

The Code of Handsome Lake combines European religious influences (especially those practiced by the Quakers) with a traditional Iroquois emphasis on family, community, and the importance of land for maintaining their culture. The largest following for Handsome Lake occurred after his death. Many Iroquois accepted rejection of alcohol and his concepts of social relationships, as well as concepts of good and evil that closely resemble Quakerism, which Handsome Lake had studied. Handsome Lake also borrowed heavily from the Iroquois Great Law of Peace, popularizing concepts such as looking into the future for seven generations and regard for the earth as mother. These ideas have since become part of pan-Indian thought across North America and, from there, were incorporated into late twentieth-century popular environmental symbolism.

The Code of Handsome Lake is still widely followed (as the Longhouse Religion) in Iroquois country. By the late twentieth century, roughly a third of the thirty thousand Iroquois in New York State attended Longhouse rites.

SEE ALSO:
Cornplanter; Hall, Louis; Iroquois Confederacy; Red Jacket; Turtle Island.

HARJO, CHITTO

SEE Crazy Snake.

HARJO, JOY (1951–)

One of the strongest voices in contemporary Native American poetry is Creek writer Joy Harjo. Harjo was born in Tulsa, Oklahoma, and she attended high school at the Institute of American Indian Arts in Santa Fe, New Mexico, and college at the University of New Mexico. She received her master of fine arts degree at the writers' program at the University of Iowa.

Harjo's 1989 book, *Secrets from the Center of the World,* and her 1990 book, *In Mad Love and War,* have received national critical attention and two prestigious awards, the William Carlos Williams Award and the Delmore Schwartz Memorial Poetry Prize. Harjo's themes often concern the Southwest, which has been her home for many years, rather than Oklahoma, where she was born and raised, but in every collection of her work there have also been poems that deal directly with Creek culture, and a Creek sensibility pervades many of her poems. In interviews, Harjo has attributed her inspiration to an old Creek woman who speaks to her and has thus become her muse. In addition to writing poetry, Harjo is also a painter, filmmaker, and musician.

Harjo's work includes *The Last Song, What Moon Drove Me to This?, She Had Some Horses, In Mad Love and War, Secrets from the Center of the World,* and *The Woman Who Fell from the Sky.* As John Scarry has pointed out in an essay on Harjo's work in the Spring 1992 issue of *World Literature Today,* Harjo's poetry often contains overlapping images, perhaps influenced by her work as a painter, that move rapidly from one world to the next: the world of dreams to the world of waking, subconsciousness to consciousness, myth to concrete experience, past to present, spiritual to physical. In fact, her poetry demonstrates the traditional idea that physical and spiritual realities are just opposite sides of the same coin. Therefore, it is not exactly correct to call Harjo's work surreal since it comes from the Indian notion that the supernatural is part of everyday concerns. As Scarry says, even though Harjo's poetry may occur in bleak landscapes filled with oppressed people, the poems show that "unity can be recovered . . . and a vision of Beauty can lead to a positive recapturing of something lost—and that all this can come to all of us at the most unlikely time and in the most unpromising place."

Being away from home seems to energize Harjo's work; many of the poems are concerned with returning home, which is much more than a geographical journey in her poetry. Home not only involves a constant journey toward the center of one's self, but also bringing the past into some kind of acceptable relationship with the present and finding a sense of what it means to be one of the people. Harjo lives and teaches in Arizona; when asked when she will return to Oklahoma, she replied that she will go back whenever she has "enough money and the right words."

Harjo recently became the fourth recipient of the Lifetime Achievement Award from the Native Writers' Circle of the Americas. She received the award at a ceremony on the campus of the University of Oklahoma in July 1995.

HARMONY ETHIC, CHEROKEE

SEE Cherokee Harmony Ethic.

HARRIS, LaDONNA (1931–)

Native American civil-rights advocate and tribal economic development specialist LaDonna Harris, a member of the Comanche Nation, was born February 15, 1931, in Cotton County, in southwestern Oklahoma. She was raised by her Comanche grand-

In addition to writing, Creek poet Joy Harjo also performs with her band, Poetic Justice.

parents and spoke only the Comanche language until beginning school at the age of six. In high school in Lawton, Oklahoma, she met Fred Harris, who became her husband. Much of LaDonna Harris's early adult life was then devoted to raising their three children and helping her husband as he went through college and law school, became an Oklahoma state senator, and then a U.S. senator. He eventually chaired the Democratic National Committee and waged two campaigns to be elected president of the United States.

Though LaDonna Harris did not attend college, from her close association with her husband's political career she received an education in government and politics that cannot be obtained in a classroom. Throughout her life, she has applied this knowledge to organizational activities on behalf of Native peoples. In recognition of her lifetime achievements and her depth of knowledge of governmental and political affairs, Dartmouth College conferred on her an honorary degree of Doctor of Laws, and she has become an educator, teaching at the Washington School of the Institute for Policy Studies.

In 1965, she gained national prominence when she played a leading role in bringing together members from Oklahoma's many diverse tribes for a series of conferences that resulted in the formation of Oklahomans for Indian Opportunity. This organization was the first to include members from all of the many Indian tribes in Oklahoma. It worked to end racial segregation of Indians in the state and to promote the achievement of equality for Native people by seeking tribal economic stability. During the late 1960s, her work with Oklahomans for Indian Opportunity led to her involvement with other organizations, including the National Rural Housing Conference, the National Association of Mental Health, and the National Committee Against Discrimination in Housing. For the National Steering Committee of the Urban Coalition, she became chair of its Health Task Force.

In 1967, President Lyndon Johnson appointed her to chair the National Women's Advisory Council of the War on Poverty, and he later appointed her to the National Council on Indian Opportunity. In 1970, she founded Americans for Indian Opportunity (AIO). She was also a founding member of the National Women's Political Caucus.

She visited indigenous peoples throughout the world as a representative of the Inter-American Indigenous Institute of the Organization of American States. President Gerald Ford appointed her to the United States Commission on the Observance of International Women's Year.

In 1975, the Harris family relocated to New Mexico at the end of Fred Harris's term of office in the United States Senate, and LaDonna Harris concentrated her efforts as president and executive director of Americans for Indian Opportunity. President Jimmy Carter appointed her as a special adviser to the director of the Office of Economic Opportunity, and she used her influence in that capacity to create an American Indian version of the Peace Corps, called the Peace Pipe Project. She then turned her attention to helping to organize the Council of Energy Resources Tribes (CERT), which assists tribes in dealing with the extraction industries (such as mining), where tribes historically have not been dealt with fairly.

Harris continues to travel widely, speaking at national and international conferences, and she also serves on the board of many organizations, among them the National Organization for Women, Save the Children, Common Cause, and the National Urban League. One of her children, Kathryn Harris Tijerina, has served as president of the Institute of American Indian Arts in Santa Fe, New Mexico.

SEE ALSO:
Council of Energy Resources Tribes.

HASKELL INDIAN NATIONS UNIVERSITY

Haskell Indian Nations University began as an Indian Training School with fourteen students on September 1, 1884. Located in Lawrence, Kansas, the school is operated by the Bureau of Indian Affairs.

Originally, three buildings made up the entire campus: a men's dormitory, a women's dormitory, and a school building. But it now has a population of about one thousand students, consists of twenty-seven buildings, and has grown from being a training school to a college to a university.

As a training school, Haskell was funded by the federal government; its early ideology was to take young Indian children and assimilate them into the mainstream Euro-American society. The institution did not have an Indian president until 1933, when Dr. Henry Roe Cloud became the president.

During the time of the government boarding schools, Haskell students, many of whom were taken unwillingly from their homes, were not allowed to speak their languages or participate in traditional customs. Oddly though, they were encouraged to perform Henry Wadsworth Longfellow's poem, "The Song of Hiawatha." "Hiawatha" was a European-American stereotype of Indian culture; participating in the performance was the only way Haskell students could be acceptably Indian.

Thomas Morgan, Indian Affairs commissioner in 1889, stated in his annual report that education should seek to disintegrate the tribes. Public schools should be used to assimilate Indians and teachers must carefully "avoid any unnecessary reference to the fact that they [the students] are Indians."

Indian parents were concerned when their children returned home without knowledge of Indian

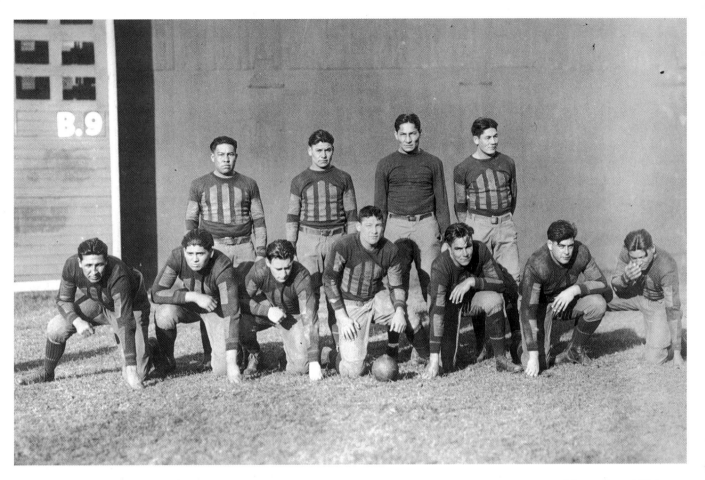

Members of the Haskell football team pose for a photo session in Boston, Massachusetts, in November 1924, before a game with Boston College.

ways, many of which included skills such as hunting and living with the earth. When the Plains Indians were confined to reservations and no longer allowed to hunt, the U.S. government issued food rations. Parents were threatened by a congressional act in 1893 that authorized the withholding of rations from parents who kept their children from school.

Many children attending the boarding schools ran away, some died from diseases and were buried in the schools' graveyards, and others committed suicide. However, some graduated and moved on to live in the mainstream society or returned home to help their people. Some of Haskell's more famous students include world renowned athletes Jim Thorpe and Billy Mills.

Today, Haskell has a group of singers and dancers who travel and perform traditional Native dances and songs. Indian, and cultural, education in general, has grown because of acknowledgment that early attempts to change Indians failed with tragic repercussions. The Bilingual Education Act of 1968, the Indian Education Act of 1972, the Indian Self-Determination and Education Assistance Act of 1975, and the Education Amendments Act of 1978 helped give Indian parents more control over money spent for the education of their children. These acts also gave Indian communities the opportunity to be involved in educational programs.

Haskell is still operated through the Bureau of Indian Affairs, but it has managed to extend its curriculum dramatically. Today, the students pay tuition, and the Indian community and students have a great deal of input into the curriculum and the operations of the university. Haskell is striving to meet the needs of the Indian students while becoming a competitive institution of higher education.

SEE ALSO:

Boarding Schools; Education, Indian; Mills, Billy; Termination Policy; Thorpe, Jim.

HATAALI

Traditional Navajo healers are called *Hataali*, or singers. Traditional Navajo medical practice treats the whole person, not just the illness, and is not conducted in isolation but in a ceremony that includes the patient's relatives. The ceremony can last from three to nine days depending upon the illness being treated and the ceremony to be performed.

Illness to the Navajos means that there is disharmony in the universe. Proper order is restored with sand paintings in a cleansing and healing ceremony. Approximately twelve hundred designs are used. Most designs can be created within the size of the average hogan floor, about six feet by six feet (almost two meters by two meters), though some are as large as twelve feet (three and one-half meters) in diameter and some as small as one foot (about thirty centimeters) in diameter. The Hataali may have several helpers in creating the intricate patterns.

There are twenty-four chantway ceremonies performed by singers. Some last up to nine days and require the assistance of dozens of helpers, especially dancers. In some ceremonies, such as the nine-day Yei-Bei-Chei, fifteen or sixteen teams of eleven members each dance throughout the night while the singer and his helpers chant prayers.

When the sand painting is ready, the patient sits in the middle of it. The singer then transforms the orderliness of the painting, symbolic of its cleanness, goodness, and harmony, into the patient and puts the illness from the patient into the painting. The sand painting is then discarded. Many years of apprenticeship are required to learn the designs of the sand paintings and the songs that accompany them, skills that have been passed down through many generations. Most Hataali are able to perform only a few of the many ceremonies practiced by the Navajos because each ceremony takes so long to learn. Sand painting is now also done for commercial purposes at public displays, but the paintings are not the same ones used in the healing rituals.

Navajos also seek medical care at the many clinics and hospitals in and near the Navajo reservation. But today, when a new health care facility is built on the reservation, it includes a room for the practice of traditional medicine by members of the Navajo Medicine Man's Association. In the 1960s, the Rough Rock Demonstration School on the Navajo reservation introduced an adult training program for Navajo medicine men.

Navajo traditional life has remained strong. In 1941, an anthropologist interviewed an entire community of several hundred Navajos and could not find even one adult over the age of thirty-five who had not received traditional medical care from a Hataali. Virtually all of the thirty-six hundred Navajos who served in World War II underwent the cleansing of the Enemyway ceremony upon their return from the war.

Large numbers of Navajos also tend to identify themselves as Christians, with most of them mixing elements of both traditional belief and Christianity. In a 1976 survey, between 25 and 50 percent called themselves Christian; this percentage varied widely by region and gender. Twenty-five thousand Navajo people belong to the Native American Church, and thousands more attend its peyote ceremonies but do not belong to the church. In the late 1960s, the tribal council approved the religious use of peyote, ending twenty-seven years of persecution. The Native American Church had originally gained a stronghold on the Ute Mountain Reservation, which adjoins the Navajo Nation on the northeast. In 1936, the church began to spread to the south into the Navajo Nation, and it grew strong among the Navajos in the 1940s.

SEE ALSO:
Indian Medicines; Native American Church; Navajo; Navajo Reservation.

HAUDENOSAUNEE

SEE Iroquois Confederacy.

HAVASUPAI

Havasupai, a corruption of the word meaning "people of the blue or green water," refers to a Yuman-speaking people living in northwestern Arizona. Controversy continues over whether the Havasupais evolved separately or were originally a break-

Barbed wire fences and modern houses contrast with the natural beauty of an ancient canyon on the Havasupai reservation in Arizona.

A Havasupai packer unloads cargo at the post office in Supai, Arizona.

away band of the Plateau People of the Hualapais. Traditionally, the Havasupai people lived by farming in Cataract Canyon and elsewhere in the Grand Canyon in the summer; they moved to camps on the Coconino Plateau during the winter in order to subsist by consuming the summer harvest, hunting, and gathering. They farmed corn, beans, sunflowers, squash, and other crops using digging sticks, hoes, and a network of irrigation ditches inside the canyon. In more recent times, cultivation of peaches, apricots, and figs supplemented traditional crops. In mid-October, families moved back to the plateau to hunt deer, antelope, and rabbits and to gather piñon nuts, mescal, and other wild plant foods. Havasupais also participated in a trade network with their neighbors, including Hopis, Navajos, Paiutes, and Hualapais.

Beginning in the late 1700s, the Havasupais had occasional contact with non-Indian explorers. Acculturation was minimal during the early years; the Havasupais simply traded for a few useful European objects. But during the late 1800s, non-Indian cattle ranchers began to invade Havasupai territory on the plateau, and miners became interested in the possible copper in the canyon.

In 1880, a reservation was established within the canyon for the Havasupais. In 1895, the Bureau of Indian Affairs founded a day school and subagency on the reservation. The Havasupais were urged to remain there year-round so that the children could attend school. This, coupled with the loss of the plateau land to cattle ranchers, disrupted the pattern of annual migrations to the plateau by Havasupais sometime in the 1940s.

The social organization of the Havasupai people was based upon the extended family living in the community of the husband's father. In their traditional society, Havasupais had no class system;

instead, status was based on individual merit, ability, and skill. Leaders were selected loosely based upon inheriting the position from one's father, but personal merit was most important. Leadership was exercised by the use of persuasion and advice by the leaders, as the men dealt with issues during visits to the sweat lodge.

The Havasupais had summer homes in the canyon and winter homes on the plateau. Winter homes were domed thatch and dirt structures over a log and pole frame. Summer homes were similar, with the addition of shade structures. Traditional clothing included shirt, breechclout, leggings, moccasins, and headband for men; and apron, long buckskin dress, moccasins, and a rabbit skin blanket for women. Basket weaving was an important craft, as baskets were used in many ways in daily life and as trade goods. Fine white buckskin was also important for trade.

The primary Havasupai ceremony has been the round dance, held annually at harvesttime. Usually Navajos, Hopis, Paiutes, and Hualapais have been invited to this feast, which is held for both social and religious purposes.

The 1996 Havasupai population is around six hundred. Their current economy is based primarily upon the tourist trade into Cataract Canyon, and horses have become important as a means to pack tourists in and out of the canyon. The tribal council is much more formalized than earlier in their history. From 1971 through 1974, the Havasupais fought to regain land that was previously theirs. Their 500-acre (200-hectare) reservation was expanded to 160,000 acres (64,000 hectares), and 95,000 acres (38,000 hectares) of Grand Canyon National Park was designated for their permanent use after Congress passed a bill that was signed into law in 1975. Since the early 1980s, their struggles for control of the land continue in court in an effort to prevent uranium companies from mining on sacred lands and in their watershed area.

SEE ALSO:
Hualapai; Yavapai.

HAWAII

The native people of the Hawaiian Islands traveled to Hawaii from the Marquesas Islands and Tahiti approximately fifteen hundred years ago. In their fight to maintain native religion and culture, and in

A lei draping on Kamehameha Day at Honolulu, Hawaii.

This statue of Kamehameha I honors the king who united the Hawaiian Islands under his rule.

terms of their battle against colonialism, native Hawaiians share a great deal in common with American Indians.

The first documented contact between Hawaiians and Europeans occurred in January of 1778 when Captain James Cook and his English crew landed on Kauai. Cook and his men encountered a feudal system with hereditary rulers. Soon afterward, one Hawaiian gained control over all of the Hawaiian Islands. After a twenty-eight-year struggle, which ended in 1810, Kamehameha I succeeded in establishing the kingdom of Hawaii.

The 1800s were a time of great upheaval for native Hawaiians. The native population of the islands was nearly three hundred thousand in 1800, but as was the case with American Indians, disease greatly reduced the population. In 1820, Protestant missionaries from New England began to arrive, and they worked against native religion and practices. In 1842, foreigners fought against the Hawaiian leadership and established a shared government, and Gerrit P. Judd became the first prime minister. In 1893, the United States deposed Queen Liliuokalani by military conquest, and a provisional government was established, which was controlled by non-Hawaiians. On June 14, 1900, Hawaii became a U.S. territory with Sanford B. Dole as its first governor. Hawaii became the fiftieth U.S. state on August 21, 1959.

In addition to its own native population, Hawaii does have American Indians who have moved there. Hawaii has 5,099 American Indian residents according to the 1990 U.S. Census, which places Hawaii forty-fourth among U.S. states in terms of Indian population. Today, native Hawaiians are attempting to regain sovereignty of their land.

Ira Hayes appeared in what is possibly the most famous image of Americans in World War II—the raising of the U.S. flag at Iwo Jima, Japan.

HAYES, IRA HAMILTON
(1923–1955)

One of the United States Marines in the famous picture of the raising of the American flag on Iwo Jima, Ira Hamilton Hayes, is best known as a World War II hero. But he is a symbol of a reluctant hero with no place in society.

Ira Hayes was born on January 12, 1923, in Sacaton, Arizona. The oldest of four sons in a farming family, he was raised in a one-room adobe home located on the Gila River Indian Reservation. He volunteered to join the marines at the outbreak of World War II. In boot camp, Hayes had to adjust

Marine Private First Class Ira Hayes in Chicago in May 1945 while on a bond-selling tour. Hayes was presented with a commission in the American Council of Indians while in Chicago.

to a very different world and was given the nickname "Chief." He expressed pride that he was the only Pima Indian to become a marine paratrooper.

In 1943, Ira Hayes sailed to Guadalcanal. His first combat was a horrible fight to take "Hellzapoppin' Ridge" from an entrenched Japanese unit. After he was reassigned as a BAR (Browning Automatic Rifleman), Hayes left with Company E for Iwo Jima in January 1945.

The United States was victorious on the eight-square-mile (twenty-one-square-kilometer) island of Iwo Jima, but it was victory at a devastating cost—over four thousand dead and fifteen thousand wounded. Hayes saw many comrades die or become injured, and it affected him deeply. During the action, a small U.S. flag was placed on the peak of Mount Suribachi, an inactive volcano, to inspire marines still fighting desperately all over the island. While climbing the volcano to run communication wire, Ira Hayes's work detail met a marine tak-

ing a larger flag up to the top. As they helped him replace the flag, Joseph Rosenthal, an Associated Press photographer, shot the picture of the six men raising the second flag, a photo that was to become nationally famous.

After Hayes was identified as one of the six flag raisers, he was reassigned to promote war bonds in the United States. Frightened by his new assignment, Hayes reluctantly returned to be greeted as a hero and receive a letter of commendation. A shy and gentle man, he was extremely uncomfortable with the publicity and felt undeserving.

After his discharge in 1945, Hayes became the object of autograph seekers, journalists, and fans who offered to buy him a drink, and he became increasingly dependent upon alcohol. In 1949, Hayes took a bit part in the film *The Sands of Iwo Jima,* and the following year, he posed for sculptor Felix De Weldon's statue of the flag raising on Iwo Jima.

In 1953, craving a new beginning out of the limelight, he enrolled in the Voluntary Relocation Program, which retrained Native Americans and relocated them to large urban areas. Ira Hayes moved to Chicago, where he was employed by International Harvester as a tool grinder. Despite his efforts to avoid the spotlight, however, this move was publicized, as was his subsequent arrest and jailing on a drunk and disorderly charge. He could not escape the public eye.

To Hayes's utter humiliation, the *Chicago Sun-Times* established a rehabilitation fund. After treatment at a sanitarium in 1953, he was given a job as chauffeur and bodyguard to a California family's children. Hayes continued to be a public figure, and after another arrest for public drunkenness, he returned to his parents' home in Bapchule, Arizona. In January 1955, he died from exposure after becoming intoxicated.

HEALING

SEE Indian Medicines.

HEALTH CARE AND HEALTH SERVICE, INDIAN

SEE Indian Health Service.

HEART OF THE EARTH SURVIVAL SCHOOL

Heart of the Earth Survival School was started in 1972 by members of the American Indian Movement and others who were concerned about dropout rates of Indian youth in public schools. The Indian youth dropout rate is among the highest in the nation, and this "survival" school was an alternative to public education with its curricula that promoted narrow, racist images of Indians and excluded Indian history from U.S. history as a whole.

Heart of the Earth based its school on being Indian and learning to survive in a non-Indian world. It also was used to make Indian youth proud of their history and heritage by developing a cultural curriculum.

The youth are not only taught about their culture and traditions, but their spiritual backgrounds, as well. Students of Heart of the Earth learn about Indian spirituality and Indian religions. They are also taught the history of the United States, not through textbooks that cover the "discovery" of America, but through texts on a history that was rich with diversity and culture, villages and roads, and trading routes already established before the Europeans invaded.

In 1994, the school began an excellence program that includes challenging accelerated academics, individualized learning, case management for students, mentor programs, job and community service placements, and eight-hour days that parallel the working day. Heart of the Earth has been so successful that it has been the model for similar schools throughout the United States and Canada.

SEE ALSO:
American Indian Movement; Benton-Banai, Edward J.; European Attitudes Toward Indigenous Peoples.

HEATHEN

Negative associations with the word *heathen* are the result of centuries of political, economic, and religious struggles, especially with regard to the spread of Christianity. *Heathen* originally referred to the Old English word that meant "heath dweller." A heath is a tract of uncultivated land overgrown with shrubs; the Native people who inhabited the heaths were also referred to as "pagans," which meant "peasant."

As the Christian religion spread throughout Europe, the word *heathen* took on a new and dangerous definition. Christians demanded allegiance to their God as "the one true God," and it was their religious duty to convert everyone to belief in their God. It was also part of their belief to have dominion, or control, over nature and all her "creatures."

The Native and tribal people who lived in more remote areas in Europe, such as the heaths, were

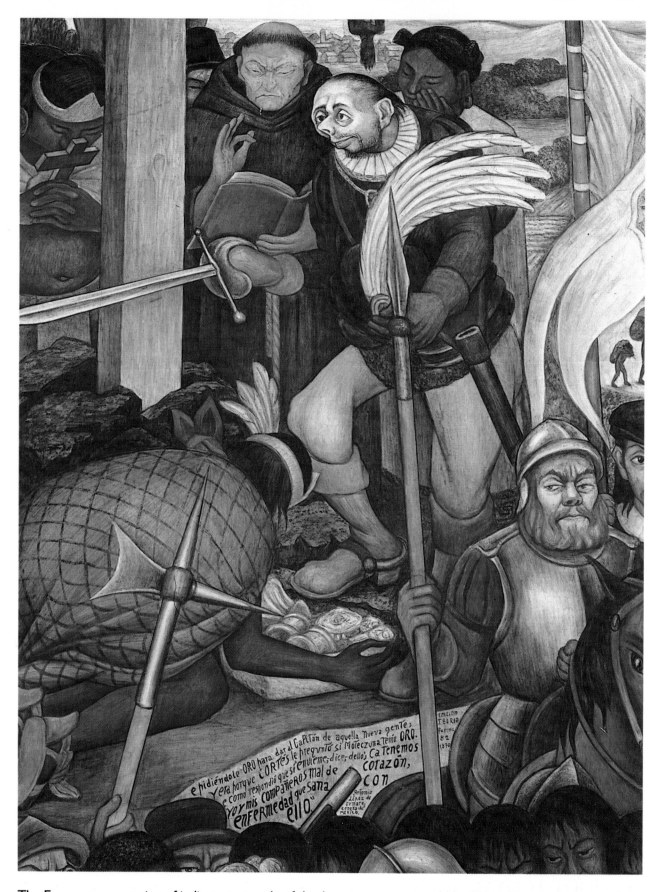

The European conception of indigenous people of the Americas, as portrayed by Diego Rivera's depiction of the arrival of Hernán Cortés in Mexico in 1519.

the last to convert to Christianity. They lived according to ancient spiritual ways that were based on the cycles of nature. Their belief that all things were spiritually alive and related to one another offended the Christians. References to "heathens" came to equal being godless or worshiping "false gods."

Because of the enormous economic and political power of the men who were the leaders of the large Christian churches, wars were waged against the so-called heathens, and large amounts of heathen lands were acquired. Those who refused to convert were killed.

By the time the continent that is now called North America was invaded, the Christians had extensive experience waging war on those who believed differently from them. Not only did the Native people of this continent base their spirituality on their relationship to nature, they looked different, and they had languages and cultures that were unfamiliar to the Christians. The Native people became known as "red-skinned heathen savages."

In order to successfully conquer any culture, two things must be upset and destroyed, the spiritual belief system and the family structure. Christianity assumed itself a superior religion and forced conversion upon Native people. Christians saw it as their duty to "save heathen souls" and to control the land base. In exchange for this "salvation," the Native people had to give up their relationship to the land, their tribal identity, their traditional family roles, and any belief that did not support Christianity. Those who resisted conversion received punishments ranging from beatings to death.

Heathen continues to be defined in modern dictionaries as "godless; worshiping false gods; a member of a people which does not acknowledge the Christian, Jewish, or Islamic God."

See also:
Christian Colonists' Views of Natives.

HEINMOT TOOYALAKET

SEE Chief Joseph.

HENDRICK (TIYANOGA)
(c. 1680–1755)

Tiyanoga, called Hendrick by the English, was a major figure in colonial affairs between 1710, when he was one of four Mohawks invited to England by Queen Anne, and 1755, when he died in battle with the French as an ally of the British. In 1754, Hendrick advised Benjamin Franklin and other colonial representatives on the principles of Iroquois government at the Albany Congress.

Hendrick, who was a member of the wolf clan, knew both Iroquois and English cultures well. He converted to Christianity and became a Mohawk preacher sometime after 1700. In England, he was painted by John Verelst and called the "Emperor of the Five Nations." Hendrick was perhaps the most important individual link in a chain of alliances that saved the New York frontier and probably all of New England from the French in the initial stages of the Seven Years' War, which in North America was called the French and Indian War (1754–1763).

Well known as a man of distinction in his manner and dress, Hendrick visited England again in 1740. At that time, King George presented him with an ornate green coat of satin, fringed in gold, which Hendrick was fond of wearing in combination with his traditional Mohawk ceremonial clothing.

A lifelong friend of Sir William Johnson, Hendrick appeared often at Johnson Hall, near Albany, where he had many opportunities to rub elbows with visiting English nobles. Sometimes he arrived in war paint, fresh from battle. Thomas Pownall, a shrewd observer of Indian affairs during the colonial period, described Hendrick as ". . . . a bold artful, intriguing Fellow and has learnt no small share of European Politics, [who] obstructs and opposes all (business) where he has not been talked to first . . . ."

Hector Saint Jean de Crevecoeur, himself an adopted Iroquois who had sat in on sessions of the Grand Council at Onondaga, described Hendrick in late middle age, preparing for dinner at the Johnson estate, within a few years of the Albany Congress: "[He] wished to appear at his very best. . . . His head was shaved, with the exception of a little tuft of hair in the back, to which he attached a piece of silver. To the cartilage of his ears . . . he attached a little brass wire twisted into very tight spirals. A girondole was hung from his nose. Wearing a wide silver neckpiece, a crimson vest and a blue cloak adorned with sparkling gold, Hendrick, as was his custom, shunned European breeches for a loincloth fringed with glass beads. On his feet, Hendrick wore moccasins of tanned elk, embroidered with porcupine quills, fringed with tiny silver bells."

At the 1754 Albany Congress that framed a colonial plan of union, Hendrick repeated the advice Canassatego had given colonial delegates at Lancaster a decade earlier. This time the conference was devoted not only to diplomacy but also to drawing up a plan for the type of colonial union the Iroquois had been requesting.

Hendrick died at the Battle of Lake George in the late summer of 1755, as Sir William Johnson

defeated Baron Dieskau. On September 8, the elderly Mohawk was shot from his horse and bayoneted to death while on a scouting party.

SEE ALSO:

Albany Plan of Union; Canassatego; French and Indian War; Iroquois Confederacy; Johnson, William.

HENRY, GORDON (1955–)

Gordon Henry is Anishinabe (also known as Chippewa or Ojibwe), from White Earth Reservation in Minnesota. He is an assistant professor of languages and literature at Ferris State University in Big Rapids, Michigan. Henry's creative work has been appearing for more than a decade in the *Earth Power Coming* anthology (1983), in *Outside White Earth* (1986), and in such journals as *Mid-American Review* (Summer 1990). In 1993, Doubleday presented an advance excerpt from Henry's novel, *The Light People*, in the *Earth Song, Sky Spirit* short-story anthology.

The Light People was then published as Volume 7 of the *American Indian Literature and Critical Studies* series of the University of Oklahoma Press. It is the story of Oskinaway, an Anishinabe who is searching for his parents—a father he barely knew and a mother "who vanished on the powwow trail." His last glimpse of her was as she got into a blue van, carrying her powwow regalia. Set in the village of Four Bears on the fictitious Fineday Reservation, the people tell Oskinaway many stories to help him in his quest. In the stories, in the mixing of fiction and poetry and of essay and myth, the story of Oskinaway unfolds amid many stories. Some of these stories are surely destined to become classics, such as the series of stories that tell how an Anishinabe's leg ended up in a museum. The book is distinguished not only for the way Henry weaves together its many different elements but also for the level of skill with which he writes in so many different forms.

Anishinabe novelist Gordon Henry, author of *The Light People*.

HENRY, PATRICK (1736–1799)

Having tried his hand and failed as a businessman and a farmer, Patrick Henry in 1760 became a lawyer. By 1763, he was known as a spellbinding speaker. In 1765, Henry was elected to the Virginia House of Burgesses as an opponent of the Stamp Act and spurred revolution in America by challenging the British to "give me liberty or give me death." Thomas Jefferson said that Henry was the best orator he had ever heard. Henry galvanized opinion in the Continental Congress and served several terms as governor of Virginia during the late 1770s and 1780s.

Patrick Henry advocated state payments to subsidize Indian-white marriages, and in the fall of 1784, he introduced such a measure into the Virginia House of Delegates. The bill directed the state to pay an unspecified sum for the marriage and an additional sum on the birth of each child. In addition, Henry proposed that Indian-white couples live tax free. Henry pushed the bill with his usual enthusiasm and oratorical flourish as it survived two readings. By the time it reached its third reading, Henry had been elected governor of Virginia. Without him in the House of Delegates, the intermarriage bill died.

Like many of the other leaders of the revolutionary movement in the English colonies, including George Washington, Henry was a speculator in the Indian lands west of the Allegheny Mountains. Because the English monarchy, by such measures as the Proclamation of 1763, had forbidden colonists from encroaching upon these Indian lands, and because Henry and other revolutionary leaders profited financially from their real estate speculations in Indian lands, Henry's appeals for "liberty" ring hollow to Native Americans. To Native Americans, the "freedom" that Henry and other revolutionary leaders sought meant the freedom to displace Native peoples from their homes, for a profit, unrestrained by the English Crown, which had attempted to recognize and protect the rights of Native peoples from the greed of English colonists. These aspects of Henry's career and his motivations are very seldom mentioned in U.S. history textbooks.

SEE ALSO:
American Revolution; Proclamation of 1763.

HENSON, LANCE (DAVID) (1944–)

Born September 20, 1944, in Washington, D.C., a member of the Southern Cheyenne Nation, Lance (David) Henson also has Oglala and French ancestry. His grandparents, Bob and Bertha Cook, raised him on a farm near Calumet, Oklahoma. Bertha Cook was a tipi maker, and Bob Cook kept the grounds for Chapter Number One of the Native American Church in Oklahoma. The last of five boys the couple raised, Henson grew up living the Southern Cheyenne culture.

After graduation from Calumet High School, Henson joined the marines and served in Vietnam. When he returned, he began writing poetry as therapy while attending the Oklahoma College of Liberal Arts (now the University of Science and Arts of Oklahoma) in Chickasha. His first book, *Keeper of Arrows*, was published in 1972 while he was a student. After graduating from college in 1972, he attended Tulsa University as a Ford Foundation Scholar, graduating in 1975 with an M.F.A. degree in creative writing. Since then he has worked as poet-in-residence in more than five hundred schools across the United States and in Europe. His poetry has been included in most of the major American Indian literature anthologies and in a wide range of magazines, including *Contact II*, *National Geographic*, *World Literature Today*, and *Studies in American Indian Literatures*.

A member of the Cheyenne Dog Soldier Society, the Native American Church, and American Indian Movement, Henson has three children—a daughter, Christian, and two sons, Jon David and Michael. Identifying with his warrior tradition, Henson has served as an official representative of the Southern Cheyenne Nation, addressing the European Free Alliance at Leewarden, the Netherlands, in 1985 and the Indigenous People's Conference at the United Nations, Geneva, Switzerland, in 1988.

Henson expresses the traditional Cheyenne vision of the world with a purity of language that is consistent with the Native value for verbal precision and conciseness. One of the few contemporary Native poets who writes and publishes bilingual poetry, Henson's knowledge of Cheyenne language and culture and his skill as both languages. Among his other books are *Another Song for America* (1987), and *Selected Poems, 1970–1983*, which was revised and published as *A Cheyenne Sketchbook* (1992). Henson's works are also included in Abenaki poet and editor Joseph Bruchac's *Survival This Way: Interviews with American Indian Poets* (1987).

SEE ALSO:

American Indian Movement; Native American Church.

Charlotte Heth, Cherokee, is a scholar in the field of Native American music.

HETH, CHARLOTTE (1937–)

Cherokee scholar Charlotte Anne Wilson Heth, a specialist in Native American music, was born October 29, 1937, in Muskogee, Oklahoma. A member of the Cherokee Nation of Oklahoma, she received a B.A. and a masters in music from the University of Tulsa. In 1975, she received a Ph.D. in ethnomusicology from the University of California at Los Angeles (UCLA). From 1976 to 1994, Heth served on the faculty at UCLA, teaching ethnomusicology. She also served as director of the American Indian Studies Center, as chair of the Department of Ethnomusicology and Systematic Musicology, and as associate dean of the School of the Arts. For two years, beginning in 1988, she was a visiting professor at Cornell University in Ithaca, New York. In 1994, she became assistant director for Public Programming at the National Museum of the American Indian at the Smithsonian Institution in Washington, D.C. She is also a linguist, being fluent in French, German, Spanish, and Cherokee.

She has edited or coedited a number of works, including *Selected Reports in Ethnomusicology* (UCLA American Indian Studies Center, 1980), *Issues for the Future of American Indian Studies: A Needs Assessment and Program Guide* (UCLA American Indian Studies Center, 1985), and *Native American Dance: Ceremonies and Social Traditions* (National Museum of the American Indian, 1992).

She has contributed to scholarly journals, including the *Chronicles of Oklahoma*, regarding

a poet using the English language have brought him national and international recognition. More than eighteen collections of his poetry have been published, including five published in Europe and translated into German, Frisian, and Italian.

In Henson's second book, *Naming the Dark: Poems for the Cheyenne* (1976), he developed themes he had introduced in *Keeper of Arrows*. These include an acknowldgment of the spiritual presence of those who have died. Many of Henson's poems are inspired by the cultural heritage of the Cheyenne in which animals such as the coyote, owl, and badger are respected as essential to human life.

In a Dark Mist (1979), written in Cheyenne and English, illustrates Henson's skill as a poet in

Native music and dance, and she contributed sections on Native music and dance to the *Native North American Almanac* (Gail Research, 1994). In 1978 she coauthored a work with Willie Jumper and Archie Sam, entitled *Music of the Sacred Fire: The Stomp Dance of the Oklahoma Cherokee* (UCLA American Indian Studies Center), and in 1992 New World Records produced her *Songs and Dances of the Eastern Indians from Medicine Spring and Allegheny*.

HEYOKA

In traditional Lakota life, men and women perform certain functions within their societies. For example, a man might be called upon to serve as a warrior, or a woman might have a special gift for healing or nursing the sick. From day to day, members of a tribe carry out their particular specialties for the benefit of all.

As observed in the nineteenth century and early twentieth century, a heyoka, pronounced "Hey-O-ka," was considered *wakan,* or sacred, a person of mystery and power whose contrary ways were a blessing. A heyoka's contrary ways often included going about his life doing everything backward, the opposite of what would be regarded as "normal." A heyoka might say "yes " when he meant "no" or "hello" when he meant "good-bye." He might ride his horse backward; complain of freezing on a hot summer day, or walk barefoot without warm clothes in the wintertime. A heyoka was a sacred clown who provided amusement and funny stories for all.

Heyokas received their power from the *wakinyan,* a thunder-being deity who lived in the West on a mountain high above the clouds. A thunder-being was thought to be the greatest power in the universe, a part of *Wakan Tanka,* or the Great Spirit. A person might become a heyoka when he or she dreamed of the thunder-being.

The heyoka tradition has almost faded during the latter half of the twentieth century, although not completely. Organizers of the Black Hills Pow-wow are looking forward to adding a heyoka dance category to the schedule of events, hoping to attract modern-day heyokas.

HIAWATHA

Hiawatha, whose dates of birth and death are uncertain but who flourished around 1570, was an Onondaga by birth, but a Mohawk by adoption. The Iroquois often adopted people from other Native and non-Native nations. It was their custom; they had no concept of disliking other people because their skin color or culture was different. The Iroquois also adopted several people of European backgrounds. They believed that anyone could take shelter under their Great Tree of Peace, as long as they did not make war on other people under the Tree.

Deganawidah, a Wyandot (Huron), and Hiawatha had a similar idea. Both wanted to stop violence among the Native peoples of the area. Both men began their quests alone and did not succeed until they combined efforts. Deganawidah and Hiawatha had to find each other and then bring the Mohawks, Senecas, Cayugas, and Oneidas to see the way of reason before they could defeat the evil wizard Tadadaho, who lived among the Onondagas. Tadadaho was said to be so powerful that birds who flew over his head died and fell at his feet. It was also said that where other men had hair, his head bore a mass of tangled snakes.

Hiawatha brought the Mohawks to agreement with his own vision of peace. After that, according to the Iroquois account, he traveled westward to confront Tadadaho. Hiawatha took his name because it means "He Who Combs," and Hiawatha was preparing to comb the snakes out of the evil Tadadaho's hair. But Tadadaho caused Hiawatha's three Onondaga daughters to sicken and die. The people, seeing that Hiawatha was suffering, came to comfort him. They even organized a game of lacrosse to entertain Hiawatha, before the Evil Wizard caused a bird to drop from the sky. The crowd pursued the falling bird and trampled Hiawatha's wife to death.

Hiawatha left the land of his birth in distress, beginning a long trek though the wilderness, during which the spirits of nature looked after him. According to the account, he crossed a lake as ducks rolled up the water to keep his feet from becoming wet. Profoundly sad during this trip, he thought that no one would console his sorrows. Alone, he knit shells into beaded patterns (later called

The historical Hiawatha was romanticized beyond recognition by Henry Wadsworth Longfellow. This painting depicts a scene from Longfellow's famous poem of the same name.

wampum) that became the Iroquois method of recording historical events and agreements.

Hiawatha's spirits were lifted when he met Deganawidah, who was still carrying on his own quest for peace. The two men both hoped that all Iroquois would come together and be of one mind.

Together, Deganawidah and Hiawatha worked to convince the Iroquois Nations that they should live in peace and adopt a council to make decisions with advice from the people. They engaged in a long struggle that went on for many years. During this time, according to the account, Hiawatha and Deganawidah approached Tadadaho three times. Only then was Tadadaho convinced, and Hiawatha was able to comb the snakes from his hair. Tadadaho's body lost its crookedness and ugliness, and Tadadaho took his seat as speaker of the new Iroquois Grand Council. *Tadadaho* became the word used to describe the head chief of the confederacy and to mean "first among equals." Tadadaho's change of heart and mind is proof to the Iroquois that peace can defeat war and good can defeat evil.

SEE ALSO:
Deganawidah; Iroquois Confederacy; Mohawk.

HICKOK, WILD BILL (1837–1876)

Born in Troy Grove, Illinois, in 1837, James Butler Hickok would later come to be known as the legendary American scout, frontier marshal, and gunfighter, Wild Bill Hickok. His numerous exploits within the rugged western frontier, particularly the tales of his gunfighting, have been exaggerated throughout the years through popular novels and movies, although his shooting abilities and daring spirit were seldom doubted.

In 1855, Wild Bill served with General James Lane's Free State forces in Kansas. He also drove stagecoaches along the Santa Fe and Oregon Trails. It was on the Oregon Trail at Rock Creek Station, Nebraska, that the well-known battle with the McCanles Gang occurred, in which David C. McCanles and two others were killed.

During the Civil War, Wild Bill served as a scout for the Union forces. In 1865, he killed an adversary in the public square of Springfield, Missouri, and was acquitted of manslaughter charges when the judge ruled that the killing was in self-defense. He later became a deputy United States marshal at Fort Riley, Kansas, where his reputation as a fearsome gunfighter increased. Although he was known to be sympathetic to the Indians of the Plains, he served with Lt. Colonel George Armstrong Custer as an Indian fighter in the bloody campaigns in the West.

After serving as a marshal in Hays City and Abilene, Kansas, Hickok toured with Buffalo Bill Cody's Wild West Show in 1872. In 1876, during a poker game in Deadwood, South Dakota, Hickok was shot from behind and killed.

SEE ALSO:
Buffalo Bill's Wild West Show; Custer, George Armstrong.

HIDATSA

The Hidatsas are a Siouan-speaking people of North America. By 1750, they lived along the upper Missouri River in what is now North Dakota. They settled in villages and, for most of the year, were primarily farmers, with corn as their major crop. Their name, *Hidatsa*, comes from the name of one of the villages.

The Hidatsas built structures of log frames and covered them with sod and thatch. In winter, after the harvest, they would leave the villages to hunt bison. During the hunt, they lived in tipis made of hide.

The Hidatsas were once closely tied to the Crow tribe but split apart from them and located near the Mandan and Arikara tribes. The Mandans referred to the Hidatsas as the Minitari. In time, the Hidatsas took on many of the Mandans' and Arikaras' religious beliefs and customs. Elaborate ceremonies, including the Sun Dance, became a large part of the Hidatsas' life.

In the nineteenth century, the tribe was made up of various societies, including the Lumpwood Society, the Stone Hammer Society, the Notched-Stick Society, the Dog Society, the Black Mouth

Wild Bill Hickok as a scout for General Philip Sheridan in the Union army during the Civil War.

Society, the Half-Shaved Head Society, and the Hot Dance Society.

Each society had distinguishing characteristics. The Lumpwood Society, for example, was strongly tied to buffalo. They prayed to buffalo for good luck. The Stone Hammer Society sought to be outstanding in battle. They thought of themselves as being made of stone and unafraid of the enemy. The Notched-Stick Society got its name from a large wooden musical instrument that was used in their ceremonies. The notches on the instrument represented a snake's backbone.

An 1883 painting by Karl Bodmer depicting a Hidatsa warrior in war dress.

The Dog Society did everything backward. They did the opposite of what was said or expressed. For example, when warriors were sent into battle to fight bravely, they were told to flee. The Black Mouth Society was made up of men who policed the villages. They painted the lower parts of their faces black and also drew a slanted black line across the entire face. They also mediated difficulties within the tribe as well as those between friendly tribes.

The Half-Shaved Head Society was so named because a member once had a vision of a buffalo with its head shaved. The Hot Dance Society's members put their hands into boiling water to get pieces of meat from the pot where it was cooking, a daring act that signified their bravery.

The Hidatsas were almost entirely wiped out by the smallpox epidemic of 1837. In 1780, the tribe had numbered twenty-five hundred. By 1804, their numbers had dropped to twenty-one hundred, and in 1900, they were less than three hundred. After the epidemic, the surviving Hidatsas moved closer to the trading post of Fort Berthold. Today, tribal members live on the Fort Berthold Indian Reservation in North Dakota. The combined population of the Hidatsas, the Mandans, and the Arikaras numbers about thirty-two hundred people.

SEE ALSO:

Arikara; Crow; Mandan.

HIGHWAY, TOMSON (1951–)

Cree playwright Tomson Highway was born in northern Manitoba, Canada, on December 6, 1951. At six, he was sent to a boarding school in The Pas, Manitoba, where he remained until he was fifteen. He then went to high school in Winnipeg and lived in a series of foster homes until he graduated in 1970.

Highway studied piano at the University of Manitoba for two years. In 1975, he graduated from the University of Western Ontario with a Bachelor of Music Honours degree. The following year, he met and worked with the renowned playwright-poet, James Reaney. For the next seven years, Highway worked with several Native organizations and traveled throughout Canada.

Highway began writing plays when he turned thirty, and, in 1986, *The Rez Sisters* was first performed. It won the Dora Mayor Moore Award for Best New Play in Toronto's 1987–1988 theater season and was also a runner-up for the Floyd S. Chalmers Award for Outstanding Canadian Play of 1986. In August 1988, the play was one of two productions to represent Canada on the main stage of the Edinburgh International Festival. In the same year, the play was a finalist for the Governor General's Award.

In 1989, Highway's next play, *Dry Lips Oughta Move to Kapuskasing,* won four Dora Mayor Moore Awards, the Floyd S. Chalmers Award for Outstanding Canadian Play of 1989, and was a finalist for the Governor General's Award for Drama. Highway has written five other plays and is a former artistic director of Native Earth Performing Arts Inc., Toronto's only professional Native theater company. In 1993, Highway received an honorary doctor of letters degree from the University of Winnipeg and the University of Western Ontario.

HILBERT, VI (1918–)

Native writer and linguist Vi Hilbert was born July 24, 1918, in Lyman, Washington. An Upper Skagit and a fluent speaker of her native Lushootseed Salish language, Hilbert has done much to ensure that her native language will be passed on to future generations. For more than fifty years, Hilbert has been recording and translating Lushootseed traditional stories. She began by interviewing elders in the Upper Skagit communities where she was reared and by listening to and transcribing and translating recordings that had been made by anthropologists twenty years earlier.

At the University of Washington in Seattle, she taught Lushootseed language and literature until her retirement in 1988. She then entered into a career as a storyteller, telling Lushootseed traditional stories bilingually, interspersing the English translation after telling each line of the story in Lushootseed. Her performances have delighted audiences throughout the continent and were a featured presentation at the Returning the Gift

Festival of nearly four hundred Native writers at the University of Oklahoma in 1992.

Her books include a textbook for instruction of her native language, titled *Lushootseed I and II*, coauthored with Thom Hess (Daybreak Star Press, 1976), and *Haboo: Native American Stories from Puget Sound* (University of Washington Press, 1985). Her work has been anthologized in such collections as *A Time of Gathering: Native Heritage in Washington State* (University of Washington Press, 1991), *A Field Guide to Seattle's Public Art* (Seattle Arts Commission, 1992), and *Peace Tales: World Folktales to Talk About* (Linnet Books, 1992). Several of her stories were also recorded in the *Parabola Storytime Series* (Harper Collins, 1992).

SEE ALSO:
Returning the Gift.

HISPANIOLA

An island located between Cuba and Puerto Rico, Hispaniola was one of the first islands visited by explorer Christopher Columbus. Nearly all of the Native American peoples who inhabited the island were killed during the half-century following Columbus's first visit in 1492.

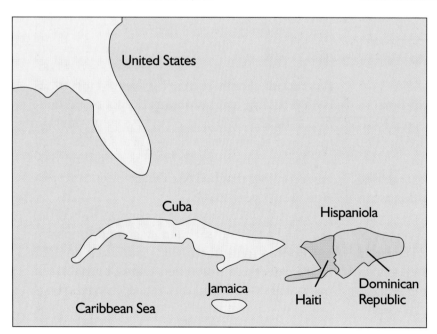

Hispaniola (now Haiti and the Dominican Republic) in relation to some of its neighbors in the Caribbean.

The Caribs, Arawaks, and other Native peoples that Columbus met during his earliest voyages were not the simple, loosely organized people he often imagined them to be. As in many other areas of the Western Hemisphere, the places that Columbus visited were thickly populated. The island chain that includes Cuba, Hispaniola, Puerto Rico, and the Bahamas was home to roughly four million people in 1492. The Native people of the islands had developed a class-stratified society, with a caste of chiefs (Tainos) at the top. Their economies had developed an intricate seaborne trade between the islands.

One of these Native groups, the Arawaks, had a social structure somewhat similar to that of the Natchez and the Pacific Northwest Coast peoples. The Arawaks, whose culture is centered in present-day Haiti, were divided into three classes: the Tainos, commoners (who paid tribute to the Tainos), and servants, who often lived and worked in the Tainos' homes. The Tainos affected an ornate style of royalty. They lived in richly appointed dwellings, wore fine woven textiles, adorned their bodies with golden ear and nose pieces, and attached brightly colored feathers to their hair. These island peoples developed into sophisticated seafarers, traveling the open ocean in dugout canoes to engage in trade or peace missions. Some of these were large enough to carry as many as thirty people. War, while known to the islanders, was rare among them.

Like many other Native American peoples, the Arawaks grew corn, their main vegetable staple. The word *maize*, an early name for corn, is derived from the Arawaks' language, as are the terms *tobacco*, *canoe*, and *hurricane*. Columbus contributed the word *cannibal* to English (through Spanish), after speculating that the Arawaks ate human flesh. But he never saw them eat it, nor did any other credible source. Scholars continue to debate over whether the word *cannibal* had any historical substance in the Arawaks' own world.

SEE ALSO:
Arawak; Caribbean, Indigenous Cultures of; Columbus, Christopher; Taino.

Students taking a break from a game of ball at a school in Santo Domingo in the Dominican Republic.

HOBSON, BARBARA (1951–)

Native educator Barbara Torralba Hobson, a member of the Comanche Nation, was born on May 26, 1951, in Lawton, Oklahoma. She graduated from high school in Lawton in 1969 and received a B.A. in psychology in 1973 from Oklahoma State University. In 1978, she received an M.A. in guidance counseling from the University of New Mexico, and in 1994, she received a Ph.D. in higher education administration from the University of Oklahoma.

From 1985 to 1988, she served as coordinator of the Native American program in the College of Engineering at the University of New Mexico. In the 1990s, she was instrumental in helping to establish a Native American studies program at the University of Oklahoma and served as the program's inaugural interim director from 1994 to 1995. Since 1995, she has served as assistant director of the program.

Hobson received national recognition in the early 1990s for her administrative skills when she served from 1990 to 1992 as project coordinator for a historic gathering of Native American creative writers from throughout the upper Western Hemisphere. The gathering, called Returning the Gift: A Festival of North American Native Writers, was a weeklong conference at the University of Oklahoma in July 1992. Planning and preparation for the conference involved some of the most prominent Native American educators, novelists, poets, playwrights, historians, and journalists from throughout Indian Country. Hobson worked for two years with festival chair Joseph Bruchac and a large steering committee to bring together the 360 Native writers who were registered for the conference, augmented by dozens of Native writers, educators, tribal leaders, and elders from the central Oklahoma region who were able to attend only some of the sessions. Funding for the conference, more than a quarter of a million dollars, was provided by many private foundations.

The conference became a highly influential event in contemporary Native literary life, leading directly to the formation of two professional organizations for Native writers. These are the Native Writers' Circle of the Americas, which annually designates by ballot a lifetime achievement honoree, and Wordcraft Circle of Native Writers and Storytellers, which conducts writing workshops for beginning and emerging Native writers and operates a mentoring program for them. The conference inaugurated an annual publication prize competition in two categories, poetry and prose, called the First Book Awards, in which emerging Native writers have an opportunity to compete for publication of their poetry or prose manuscripts by a participating press. Enthusiasm for Native theater and the large number of Native playwrights at the conference led to the inauguration of the *Native Playwrights Newsletter*.

Many publications have resulted from the Returning the Gift conference, including an anthology of original creative work by festival participants, published by the University of Arizona Press in 1994 and titled *Returning the Gift: Poetry and Prose from the First North American Native Writers' Festival*. A 1993 anthology of Southwest Native literary work, entitled *Neon Powwow*, from Northland Publishing in Flagstaff, Arizona, was a direct result of ideas generated by participants at the conference, as was *Aniyunwiya/Real Human Beings: An Anthology of Contemporary Cherokee Prose,* from Greenfield Review Press in 1994. An anthology of Navajo writing is in production, as are numerous other works resulting from the conference. In the years since the conference, publishers and editors of Native literary publications have been busy publishing the work of writers they met at the conference, while the Native writers, in turn, have been busy submitting their work to the many publications throughout Indian Country that they first learned about at the conference.

In successive years, the Returning the Gift conference has become an annual regional gathering. In 1993, it was a Southwest regional conference, again at the University of Oklahoma. In 1994, it was a Pacific Northwest regional conference, on the Makah Reservation on the Pacific Coast in Washington. In 1995, it was Midwest regional conference, hosted by the Oneida Nation of Wisconsin at Green Bay. In 1996, it will again be a larger gathering of writers from throughout Indian Country, hosted by the En'owkin Centre of the Okanogan Nation in Penticton, British Columbia, Canada.

The Returning the Gift conference in 1992 was intended to be an opportunity for Native creative

Barbara and Geary Hobson, of the University of Oklahoma, played important roles in organizing a large gathering of Native literary writers called Returning the Gift: A Festival of North American Native Writer in July 1992.

writers to meet and network with one another, a goal that has succeeded beyond all expectations. Hobson's administrative skills in organizing the conference are today recognized as one of the reasons it has proven to be a historic event in Native literary life.

SEE ALSO:
First Book Awards; Hobson, Geary; Returning the Gift.

HOBSON, GEARY (1941–)

Native writer and educator Geary Hobson, of Cherokee, Quapaw, and Chickasaw descent, was born June 12, 1941, in Chicot County, Arkansas. He graduated from Desha Central High School in Rohwer, Arkansas, in 1959. After serving in the United States Marine Corps, he received a B.A. in

English in 1968 and an M.A. in English in 1969 from Arizona State University. In 1986, he received a Ph.D. in American studies from the University of New Mexico.

Hobson has taught at the University of New Mexico, the University of Arkansas at Little Rock, and Central Arkansas University at Conway. He is presently associate professor of English at the University of Oklahoma. While at the University of New Mexico, he coordinated the Native American studies program. He speaks a number of languages, including Cherokee, Spanish, and French. Since the early 1980s, he has been active in the restoration of Arkansas Quapaw tribal status, and he has served as a member of the tribal council of the Arkansas Band of Quapaw Indians.

In 1979, Hobson edited *The Remembered Earth: An Anthology of Contemporary Native American Literature*. This was one of the first collections of a vibrant literature being produced largely by university-educated Native people; it is widely regarded as one of the best anthologies of Native literature. Originally published by Red Earth Press, the anthology is now available from the University of New Mexico Press. In 1990, Hobson published *Deer Hunting and Other Poems* (Strawberry Press), a collection of some of his finest poetry.

His poems, stories, essays, and reviews have appeared in many publications, among them *Arizona Quarterly*, *Contact/II*, *Greenfield Review*, *Quilt*, *Slackwater Review*, *Telescope*, *Y'Bird*, *Beloit Poetry Journal*, and *World Literature Today*. His work has also appeared in a number of anthologies, including *Songs from This Earth on Turtle's Back*, *The Clouds Threw This Light*, and *OYO: An Ohio River Anthology*. From 1975–1976, he served as editor of *New America*. His poetry has been translated and published abroad in Serbo-Croatian and in Dutch. Among his works in progress is a critical and literary history of American Indian and Native Canadian writing and publishing from 1968 through 1990.

In the late 1980s, Hobson began serving on the steering committee, as project historian, for the Returning the Gift conference of Native writers, which was held at the University of Oklahoma in 1992. In 1990 his wife Barbara became project coordinator for the conference. In the anthology commemorating the gathering, entitled *Returning the Gift: Poetry and Prose from the First North American Native Writers' Festival* (University of Arizona Press, 1994), he contributes an essay recounting the history of the conference, which has proven to be an important event in contemporary Native American literature.

Since 1992, when the Native Writers' Circle of the Americas was formed at the Returning the Gift conference, Hobson has administered the national office of the organization at the University of Oklahoma, which conducts the annual balloting for the Lifetime Achievement Award. He and Barbara Hobson also now organize the annual awards banquet at the University of Oklahoma, where the recipient of the Lifetime Achievement Award and the recipients of the First Book Awards in poetry and in prose, are honored. The Lifetime Achievement Award honorees have been as follows: 1992, N. Scott Momaday (Kiowa and Chero-

kee); 1993, Simon J. Ortiz (Acoma Pueblo); 1994, Leslie Marmon Silko (Laguna Pueblo); and 1995, Joy Harjo (Muscogee, or Creek).

SEE ALSO:
First Book Awards; Hobson, Barbara; Returning the Gift.

HOGAN

A family dwelling, the hogan is a distinctive type of Navajo architecture. Its design evolved largely as a result of available construction materials and the influence of building techniques from other cultures that the Navajos have adapted to suit their needs.

The earliest type of hogan, and the one most prevalent when the Navajos began to come into contact with Europeans, is a pole-and-earth structure known as a forked-stick hogan. It has a foundation of three long poles that are set upright like a tripod, with crotches that interlace at the top, somewhat like a tipi. A doorway, facing the east, is framed with more poles to form a small rectangular vestibule, or entryway, and a smoke hole is left open in the wall above the door. There are no other openings and no windows. The frame is covered with slender poles and then a layer of bark. Finally, the entire structure is covered with earth, making a compact structure to give protection from the elements.

The forked-stick hogan blends so well with its surroundings that one of the first Spaniards to comment upon the Navajos, Fray Alonso de Benavides, stated in 1634 that the Navajos lived underground, apparently mistaking the earth-covered huts for tunnels bored into the hills. In 1788, another Spaniard, Vicente Tronosco, described a visit to the land of the Navajos: "They took me to one of their houses (the construction of which is of earth and wood resembling a campaign tent except that it has a kind of vestibule or small square room at the entrance) in which I was lodged."

Archaeologists have attempted to date the construction of forked-stick hogans by using the tree ring dating method (dendrochronology) to determine when the timbers were cut for the main

A Navajo hogan in Canyon de Chelly, Arizona.

The hogan in this photo was abandoned after the death of its owner. It will not be reoccupied, and its furnishings will not be disturbed.

frames. However, not many timbers survive from earlier times, and the mid-sixteenth century is the earliest date obtained so far from a forked-stick hogan timber, from the Gobernador drainage of the upper San Juan River.

The forked-stick hogan had very little in the way of furniture. For easy storage, clothing, bedding, and possessions were easily hung from hooks on the walls. A cooking fire in the center of the structure provided warmth.

The circular shape of the hogan has significance in Navajo culture. Many Navajo ceremonials can only be conducted inside a circular structure. During the Spanish colonial era, Navajos also built circular hogans constructed of stone masonry. These were built with cribbed roofs similar to the technique used by the Pueblos in building kivas, the underground chambers in their pueblos. The fitted stone masonry techniques also give evidence of Pueblo influence.

After the Navajo Long Walk and internment by the United States Army at Bosque Redondo in east-

ern New Mexico from 1864 to 1868, the Navajos found new building materials and construction techniques after they returned to their homeland. Six-sided hogans began to be constructed entirely of logs notched and fitted at the corners, creating a large, circular room. The length of the logs in the exterior walls was the same as railroad ties, showing the influence of railroad construction in the West. The roofs were cribbed in the manner of the stone hogans. Later, hogans began to be built of beams obtained from sawmills rather than untrimmed logs.

Navajos also began building rectangular log houses after their return from Bosque Redondo, but since they were not suitable for ceremonials, they were not a popular design. American-style wood frame houses began appearing in the twentieth century, but like the rectangular log cabins, their design did not satisfy the cultural needs of the Navajos. Where frame houses appeared, the family almost always also had a hogan nearby. Often, the family continued to live in the hogan and used the frame house for storage. Increasingly, however, Navajos are adopting Native American architectural patterns for housing, while maintaining and sharing hogans for ceremonial use.

Many surveys by sociologists have been conducted throughout the Navajo Nation at intervals during the twentieth century, documenting the percentage of Navajos who live in hogans and the percentage who live in frame houses. In the 1950s, hogans continued to be the most common kind of dwelling throughout the nation, but there was wide variation from community to community. In Fort Defiance and Shiprock, frame houses had replaced hogans almost entirely. In Tuba City, Dinnebito, and Klagetoh hogans predominated by percentages ranging from 58 to 87 percent, while in Tonalea, all permanent dwellings surveyed were hogans. Similar studies in 1970 and 1974 also found wide variations from community to community, but overall the percentage of Navajos living in hogans throughout the nation had dropped to 31 percent in the 1970 study and to 16 percent in the 1974 study. However, even in communities where housing had shifted entirely from hogans to frame houses, at least one hogan was maintained by the community for ceremonial use.

Shifts in Navajo residential patterns have also affected housing. Increasingly, young Navajo couples have wanted the conveniences associated with urban life and to live near schools and employment opportunities. The Navajo Housing Authority and the Navajo Tribal Utilities Authority have helped make this possible by engaging in the construction of housing projects in these locations.

— D. L. Birchfield

SEE ALSO:
Architecture, Indian; Bosque Redondo; Long Walk, Navajo; Navajo; Pueblo.

A hogan adds an accent to the landscape at the Navajo Nation in Shiprock, New Mexico.

HOGAN, LINDA (1947–)

Chickasaw poet, novelist, and essayist Linda Hogan was born on July 16, 1947, in Denver, Colorado. As a child, she was influenced by her uncle, Wesley Henderson, who was active in the White Buffalo Council. After receiving an M.A. in English and creative writing in 1978 from the University of Colorado, she helped organize the Colorado Cultural Program and began working at the Denver Indian Center. Since 1984, she has been a member of the board of directors of the Denver Indian Center.

In 1979, she was poet-in-the-schools in both Colorado and Oklahoma. From 1981 to 1984, she was assistant professor in the Tribes Program at Colorado College in Colorado Springs, Colorado. From 1982 to 1984, she was associate professor of American and American Indian studies at the University of Minnesota. She is presently associate professor of Native American and American studies at the University of Colorado.

Hole-in-the-Day (Younger) was assassinated before he could move to the White Earth Reservation in Minnesota, which was created by a treaty in 1867 that he helped to negotiate.

HOLE-IN-THE-DAY (YOUNGER) (BUGONEGIJIG) (1825–1868)

Hole-in-the-Day (Younger) was the son of Ojibwe (Chippewa) leader Hole-in-the-Day (Elder). The son's principal concern was making war against the Sioux, the traditional enemies of the Ojibwes. Aided by firearms provided by white traders, Hole-in-the-Day (whose name actually means Opening-in-the-Sky) played a major role in pushing the Sioux westward from their former lands near the Great Lakes. At one point, the battles between the Sioux and Ojibwes became so violent that the U.S. Army intervened to set boundaries.

The younger Hole-in-the-Day became head chief of the Ojibwe Bear Clan in 1846, after his father died. He visited Washington, D.C., several times and at one point married a non-Native newspaper reporter there. He was known as a bargainer and a person who was not afraid to take his cut of any agreement on behalf of his people.

While many Ojibwes complained that Hole-in-the-Day was aggrandizing himself at the expense of his people, he became rich. He was politically prudent, however, and distributed benefits to enough people to gain popular support from "progressive" Ojibwes. When his people were compelled to move to the White Earth reservation in northern Minnesota, Hole-in-the-Day at first refused to go. He later relented, however, just before he was killed by his own people at Crow Wing, Minnesota.

SEE ALSO:
Ojibwe.

HOLLAND

SEE Dutch Colonists.

HOLLYWOOD, INDIANS, AND INDIAN IMAGES

In the film world, Indians have been viewed through strangely colored lenses, lenses that distort their true images. Throughout the twentieth century, the motion picture industries have been largely responsible for shaping images of American Indians for the general public, images that have been sadly lacking in any authenticity or respect to American Indians and their many diverse cultures.

There were as many as five hundred pictures produced each year during 1933 to 1946, now considered the heyday of the B (low-budget) western. And it was within this particular period that the worst damage was done in perpetuating outlandish and ridiculous stereotypes of American Indians. These films were never concerned with accurately portraying the over four hundred distinct tribes comprising the First Peoples of America. Nor were these films ever interested in depicting American Indians as *people*—but rather as cutout caricatures with no resemblance to anything even remotely human.

The strong religious, family, and cultural life of American Indians has been disregarded and ridiculed beyond recognition. The motion picture industry has successfully placed in the minds of the public a permanent fiction about American Indians. While Native people and advocates have made great strides in trying to erase these images, they still pervade the world.

Many of these images consistently nurtured by the movie industry include the idea that Native peoples are quaint, simpleminded, and "not quite human." Native peoples were often portrayed as savages who visited the most fiendish acts of cruelty upon the "white man." Stereotypes cultivated by the movie industry have included the Indian as drunken clown; the ignoble and noble savage; the heathen; the proud and stoic Indian brave or chief; the mystical medicine man; the perpetual loser in society; the wild or crazy red man; and, most recently, the saint, intent upon preserving harmony in the world.

Native women have been portrayed as lowly "squaws"—usually anonymous, quiet figures who live in the background. In the Hollywood version, their lives consist largely of maintaining the family home, which is nearly always, and thus often inaccurately, portrayed as a tipi, and of taking care of her "papoose"—a very young child usually bundled up and strapped to a cradle board. As is so often the case with stereotypical images,

A movie still from Columbia Picture's 1952 release *Son of Geronimo*. Many critics point out that Hollywood cannot be accused of intentionally distorting Indian history, because to intentionally distort something requires a knowledge of it.

these portrayals of women and children may contain ingredients, such as the tipi, that are true of certain cultures but that lose their authenticity when they are applied, as Hollywood often did, to all Native cultures and peoples.

The earliest depictions of American Indians in film were largely influenced by the extravagant Wild West shows, popular dime novels, and stage dramatizations of the late nineteenth and early twentieth century. One of the first known silent films about American Indians was called *The Sioux Ghost Dance*, which was produced in 1894 by the (Thomas) Edison Studios. This began the era of the silent film; literally hundreds of films depicting Indians were produced. Most notable of these were the films *The Squaw Man* (1914), *Braveheart* (1925), and *The Vanishing American* (1925).

One of the most notable filmmakers in the early days of film was John Ford. He was twenty-nine years old when he directed *The Iron Horse* in 1924

and from then on directed other films such as *Stagecoach* (1939), *Drums Along the Mohawk* (1939), *She Wore a Yellow Ribbon* (1949), and *Cheyenne Autumn* (1964). Though heralded in his time and a recipient of several awards, John Ford has been criticized for his presentation of American Indians.

Films produced during the 1950s reflected the federal government's encouragement of Indian assimilation into American society. Some films produced during this time were *Broken Arrow* (1950), *The Last Hunt* (1955), and *The Searchers* (1956). Also, the TV series *The Lone Ranger*, featuring Jay Silverheels as Tonto, the Lone Ranger's "faithful Indian companion" and sidekick, was popular.

In the 1970s, films were produced that were sympathetic to the Native Americans' point of view and also challenged the U.S. involvement in the Vietnam War. These movies included *Little Big Man* (1971), *Soldier Blue* (1970), and *Ulzana's Raid*

(1972). The 1970s also marked a decline in the popularity of westerns, and Native Americans started to appear in movies that challenged main-stream values, such as *Harry and Tonto* (1974) and *One Flew Over the Cuckoo's Nest* (1974). American television began airing pro-Indian sagas such as "I Will Fight No More Forever" (ABC, 1975), "Mystic Warrior" (ABC, 1984), and "Roanoke" (PBS, 1986).

It was during this time that the movement for Indian self-determination began at full force in North America in general—and in Hollywood. The noted Creek actor Will Sampson (1934–1987) founded the American Indian Registry in 1983. This organization encourages the film industry to give Native actors more opportunities—resulting in more visibility for Natives in motion pictures than ever before. This is a positive step for Hollywood, which has a long history of casting non-Natives wearing dark greasepaint and nose putty to portray Indians.

One of the most widely acclaimed films produced was *Dances With Wolves* (1990). Though it received several Academy Awards and furthered the careers of talented Native American actors, some critics argue that it only perpetuated the romantic myth of Indians as noble savages. The film also carried on the Hollywood tradition of por-

This poster advertises an episode from the serialized motion-picture version of *The Lone Ranger,* featuring Tonto, the Lone Ranger's "faithful Indian companion."

traying a white man's view of the Indians—with Indians as convenient background props.

The movie industry's treatment of American Indians harms viewers, especially youth. Film is a powerful medium, and young people draw many of their impressions from motion pictures and television. The ethnic stereotypes promoted in film and other media have the power to profoundly influence attitudes toward people throughout society; the most impressionable are the children. It has been common for even American Indian children watching a "cowboys and Indians" movie to, invariably, cheer for the cavalry. Today, the era of the B western movie is over, and the motion picture industries have gained new insight into what is appropriate and what is not. Moviemakers are much more sensitive to issues surrounding the portrayal of American Indians than just a few decades ago.

Despite this relatively recent sensitivity to Native American people and their concerns, stereotypes and misrepresentations of American Indians still prevail. Even the popular Walt Disney animated motion picture *Pocahontas* (1995) has not escaped scrutiny by some critics, despite the fact that Disney made efforts to include Native American technical advisers and actors to provide the voices of the Indian characters.

Today, more and more Native Americans are producing and creating their own films. These independent works are providing audiences with views and perspectives on Indian cultures right from the source, rather than through Hollywood's unjust interpretations.

— T. Midge

SEE ALSO:
European Attitudes Toward Indigenous Peoples; Noble Savage; Scalping; Westerns, Portrayals of Indians in.

SUGGESTED READINGS:
Aleiss, Angela. "In the Land of Hollywood Make-Believe Anyone Can Say They're Indian," *Indian Cinema Entertainment*, Winter, 1995.

Calder, Jenni. *There Must Be a Lone Ranger*. New York: Taplinger Publishing Company, 1974.

Friar, Natalie, and Ralph Friar. *The Only Good Indian: The Hollywood Gospel*. New York: Drama Book Specialist/Publishers, 1972.

French, Philip. *Westerns*. New York: Oxford University Press, 1977.

Hirschfelder, Arlene B. *American Indian Stereotypes in the World of Children*. Metuchen, N.J.: The Scarecrow Press, Inc., 1982.

O'Connor, John E. *The Hollywood Indian: Stereotypes of Native Americans in Film*. Trenton: New Jersey State Museum, 1980.

HOMOSEXUALITY

Problems facing gay and lesbian Indian people include some of the same issues facing the gay community at large: absence of civil rights in a country that has granted citizenship rights to other minorities decades ago; homophobia, including violent acts against and even killings of gays and lesbians; and the military ban on homosexuals. Lesbian and gay Indians, however, face difficulties on two main fronts—the ongoing Indian struggle for survival on the tribal and individual level combined with the quest of the gay community for dignity and equal opportunities. Coming-out for an Indian young person is especially frightening because the possibility of rejection from friends and tribal members, for a person whose identity is based in the community, is especially devastating.

Though it is hard to generalize, many Indian communities treat homosexuality with a "don't ask, don't tell" attitude. The white gay community might interpret this attitude as homophobic. But it may be positive within the communities in which it occurs; in traditional Indian society, not everything needs to be analyzed and talked to death. Some things are simply accepted as is.

In traditional cultures, there were often specific social and ceremonial roles for gay people and respect for their sexual orientation, which was believed to be a powerful one that allowed them to see from both the male and female worlds. Yet because of Christianizing influences, it cannot be denied that there is a good deal of homophobia in most Indian communities today.

Growing up with dominant culture influences—the double misrepresentation of Indians as a conquered and vanquished people and homosexuals as freaks and castaways—is especially harmful in terms of erasing the young Indian gay's or lesbian's sense of self-worth. Many Indian gays and lesbians move to large urban areas, and yet they do not always feel completely comfortable in the gay community, which still has a long way to go toward the acceptance of minorities and the celebration of diversity. The gay community continues to perpetuate images of whiteness as its ideal. This lack of acceptance has led to such groups as GAI, Gay American Indians, founded in San Francisco in 1975 by Northern Paiute Randy Burns and Lakota Barbara

Cameron, as well as groups in New York City, Minneapolis, Seattle, and Nashville.

One problem facing the gay Native community is underreporting of Indians with AIDS. GAI in San Francisco has lost 33 members to AIDS since 1985, and yet the Centers for Disease Control counted only 448 Native Americans with AIDS nationally as of December 1992. These numbers come from Indian Health Service (IHS),which only serves 42 percent of all Native people. IHS is seriously underfunded for AIDS treatment. In California, a state with many lesbian and gay people, especially in San Francisco and Los Angeles, many local and state health departments do not even have a Native American–Alaska Native category on their statistics sheets. This limits the visibility of Indians with AIDS. In some cases, it is difficult for Indian people with AIDS to return home to their reservations when they are ill and need attention because of homophobia in their communities. Groups like GAI are struggling to make Indian communities aware of traditional roles for gay people that allow for more freedom because of their spirit-based view of gender.

SEE ALSO:
AIDS; Berdache.

HOPEWELL CULTURE

Hopewell is a name archaeologists have given to a culture of Indian mound builders that succeeded the Adena Culture in the eastern woodlands. It is not known if the Hopewells were descendants of the Adenas or if they were a new people who had moved into the Ohio River Valley and adjacent areas. Adena Culture had reached its peak by 100 B.C.E. and had entered into its decline. At the same time, Hopewell Culture was beginning to flourish. Hopewell Culture entered its decline by 400 C.E., though it may have lasted until 600 C.E. in some areas.

The Hopewells built larger, more elaborate burial mounds than the Adenas as well as larger geometric patterns of earthworks that frequently enclose the mounds. A typical Hopewell mound might be forty feet (twelve meters) high and one hundred feet (thirty meters) across at the base. Other earthen structures, in the form of circles, squares, rectangles, and octagons, are sometimes as much as 1,600 feet (485 meters) in diameter.

The Hopewells, like the Adenas, enclosed many artifacts in their burial mounds, but their items were more elaborate and more artistic than those made by the Adenas. Hopewell artisans were very skilled at hammering large nuggets of copper into the shape of tools, such as axes and awls, an art form learned from the Adenas. The Hopewells flattened pieces of copper into animal shapes or in the form of human hands, as well as other shapes, to be worn as ornaments, and heavy flattened sheets of copper were made into breastplates. Other copper artifacts included beads, pipes, pendants, and gorgets, or ornamental collars. An elaborate headdress in the shape of a pair of antlers, made from copper, was found in one burial site. The Hopewells also hammered gold and silver into thin sheets of foil and used them to cover objects carved from bone and antler. They collected fragments of meteors containing lead and hammered them into various ornamental shapes, and they possessed great skill at carving items from stone. Unlike the Adenas, the Hopewells also excelled at making pottery.

Many Hopewell artifacts, including some of the finest pottery, seem to have been made only to be placed in graves, which created a continuous demand for raw materials to make the luxury items. The demand for these items caused the Hopewells to create a trade network that extended throughout much of the North American continent east of the Rocky Mountains. Traders helped distribute Hopewell ideas into areas outside of their core area in Ohio, including the idea of building mounds, which spread through much of the eastern woodlands. Archaeologists have found more than a dozen variants of the Hopewell Culture. These distant centers continued to flourish, scattered throughout the eastern woodlands, for as long as the Hopewells were able to maintain their trade network.

The Hopewell trade network brought raw materials to Ohio from far away—obsidian from the far West, conch shells and shark teeth from the Gulf Coast, and the teeth and claws of grizzly bears from the Great Plains and the Rocky Mountains. This trade network began breaking down about 400 C.E. as Hopewell Culture declined.

Hopewell influences led to the development of an Effigy Mound culture in a region now consisting of the states of Iowa, Minnesota, and Wisconsin. After Hopewell Culture declined, this Effigy Mound culture continued for several centuries. Their effigy mounds are often burial mounds, but they are also large pieces of artwork constructed of earth. Unlike the Hopewells, these mounds rarely contain burial artifacts. The Effigy Mound culture of the upper Midwest constructed many effigy mounds in the form of bears, panthers, birds, and even humans. One bird effigy near Madison, Wisconsin, has a wingspan of 625 feet (190 meters). Both the Adena and Hopewell Culture are known to have constructed some effigy mounds, and the Great Serpent Mound, the largest of all the effigy mounds, in southwestern Ohio, is thought to be of either Adena or Hopewell origin.

No one knows why the Hopewell Culture declined, but it would be another four hundred years, in about 800 C.E., before another great cultural tradition, the Mississippian, would begin to rival its accomplishments. During the interim, Indian cultures became more localized and diversified, and the peoples' energies were channeled into building fortifications rather than mounds, an indication that the breakup of Hopewell Culture had led to warfare between different groups.

— D. L. Birchfield

SEE ALSO:

Adena Culture; Mississippian Culture; Mound Builders; Serpent Mound.

HOPI

The Hopis are a Pueblo people of the Southwest whose language is a member of the Uto-Aztecan family. Their reservation of approximately 1.5 million acres (600,000 hectares) in present-day northeastern Arizona is completely surrounded by the Navajo reservation. The Hopis have never entered into a treaty with the United States. Their reservation was created in 1882 by executive order of

More than just artistic creations, the Hopi Clan Rocks, near Moenave, Arizona, are symbols of enduring tribal and cultural traditions.

the U.S. government. Historically, the Hopis embraced a much larger area than their present reservation, though for many centuries their population has been concentrated on a succession of mesas near the center of their land.

An agricultural people, the Hopis have much in common with the Pueblo peoples of New Mexico. But they do not participate in the All-Indian Pueblo Council, and their culture, language, and identity as a people are distinctly separate. Today, there are more than nine thousand Hopis, giving them a population larger than most of the pueblos of New Mexico.

The term *pueblo* is rarely applied to the Hopi settlements, which are instead usually called villages. Some of the villages of the Hopis may be the oldest continuously occupied settlements within the present boundaries of the United States. They are thought to date from about 1100 C.E., possibly earlier, and only the pueblo of Acoma, in New Mexico, might be as old. The Hopi villages and the pueblo of Acoma share something else in common, along with the pueblos of Zuni, Taos, and Picuris in New Mexico. They are the only settlements of Pueblo peoples that had not been moved by the Spanish between 1598 and 1700. Picuris pueblo was abandoned during the eighteenth century, but the others are still in the same locations where the Spanish found them when

This doll is a gift of the Kachina spirit dancers to a two-year-old Hopi child. The giving of gifts occurs on the annual visit of the Kachina spirits from their homes in the San Francisco Mountains, north of Flagstaff, Arizona.

they began colonizing New Mexico in 1598. This stability and maintenance of their ties to their ancestral homeland have helped the Hopis maintain their culture.

This Hopi woman is in dance regalia at the Santa Fe Indian Market, in Santa Fe, New Mexico.

Hopis are among the most skilled dry farmers in the world. Pictured above is a cornfield of the Eagle Clan of the village of Oraibi in the Hopi Nation in Arizona.

Isolation from the centers of the Spanish colonial population also helped the Hopis, as the degree of stress on their traditional life was less than that suffered by the Pueblo peoples of New Mexico. Despite this relative isolation from Spanish colonizers, however, Hopis, whom the Spanish called Moquis, were visited by just about every Spanish expedition into the Southwest, beginning with the Coronado expedition in 1540, and each expedition disrupted their lives to some extent. The degree of disruption increased dramatically once the Spaniards colonized the region in 1598.

The Spanish found the Hopi villages occupying four mesa tops. The Hopis practiced dry farming in the arid valleys beneath the mesas. One of the mesas has been abandoned, and the remaining ones are known as First Mesa, Second Mesa, and Third Mesa. The oldest villages, including Old Oraibi and Shangopavi, are on the first two mesas, while the newest mesa-top village, Hotevilla, was constructed in 1906. It was hastily built by Hopi

women whose men had been incarcerated by the United States and sent to Alcatraz Island in San Francisco Bay to prevent them from moving to Utah. Today, at the foot of each of the three mesas, are three modern Hopi communities. Many Hopis, however, prefer to live in ancient villages on top of the mesa, despite the lack of modern conveniences in many of the dwellings. The Hopis also have a cultural center with a restaurant and motel, but a guide is required before entering the villages.

Traditional government among the Hopis, like their Pueblo neighbors in New Mexico, features leadership from different sources of strength within each community. Clans are an important source of providing leadership. Among some Pueblo peoples, specific clans have traditional obligations to provide leadership. Among the Hopis, the Bear Clan has this responsibility. Among Pueblo peoples, religion encompasses many things that Europeans and Americans associate with government. Among the Hopis, for example, a religious leader

This Hopi potter is firing her pottery in a manner practiced by the Hopis for unknown generations. First Mesa can be seen in the background.

called a kikmongwi has serious responsibilities to the people. With the help of assistants, the kikmongwi performs ceremonies and many other traditional duties, such as organizing hunts and the planting of crops. Both the Spanish and the United States tried to subvert traditional Hopi government and religion. The imposition by the United States of a tribal council as a national form of government is viewed by many Hopis as a foreign-imposed system. It has caused some friction in Hopi traditional life. But on the whole, the Hopis have adjusted to the demands of the colonizers while still maintaining their culture.

The end of the nineteenth century and the early years of the twentieth century were a difficult period for the Hopis. This is when the United States attempted to force acculturation upon the Hopi people. The method of choice was the boarding school, where Hopi children were isolated from their families and were forbidden to speak their native language. Army troops were used on occasion to forcibly remove Hopi children from their villages. Some Hopis were in favor of having their children undergo the process that Americans called "education," thinking it might help their people survive the intrusions of the colonizers into their lives. Much of the training, however, involved little more than indoctrination in European agricultural practices, while child labor was used to maintain the schools. Other Hopis were bitterly opposed to having their children taken from them and to the arrogant attitudes of United States officials and missionaries.

These different factions among the Hopis came to be known as the Friendlies (those who were disposed toward attempting to adjust their lives to the demands of the colonizers) and the Hostiles (those who were opposed to all intrusions into their traditional life). When friction reached a crisis level in one Hopi village, the disharmony was resolved by a tug of war. The winners remained in the village, and the losers moved to another location.

Today, Hopi traditional life remains strong. Kachinas, a form of spirit beings, visit the Hopis annually for six months, during which the Hopi ceremonials take place. The Kachinas are said to live in the San Francisco peaks, near Flagstaff, Arizona, which are sacred mountains to the Hopis. The Kachinas arrive in the villages during the Bean Dance each year in February.

In literature and the arts, Hopis have distinguished themselves among Native peoples. Hopi-Miwok writer Wendy Rose, who is coordinator of Indian Studies at Fresno City College in California, has held positions with the Women's Literature Project of Oxford University Press, with the Smithsonian Institution Native Writers' Series, with the Modern Language Association Commission on Languages and Literature of the Americas, and with the Coordinating Council of Literary Magazines. Her books include *Hopi Roadrunner Dancing*; *Long Division: A Tribal History*; *Academic Squaw: Reports to the World from the Ivory Tower*; *Lost Cop-*per; *What Happened When the Hopi Hit New York*; *The Halfbreed Chronicles*; *Going to War with All My Relations*; and *Bone Dance*.

Hopi producer-director Victor Masayesva, Jr., has created a feature-length film, *Imagining Indians*, that succeeds in conveying Native American resentment toward the use and exploitation of Native cultures for commercial purposes. *Imagining Indians* is a ninety-minute film that explores the commercial appropriation of Native stories, rituals, and objects, examining what happens when they become commercial commodities. The film is part movie and part documentary. It is interspersed with clips of Hollywood classics that depict Indian stereotypes and with interviews with Indian extras and crew members from the sets of *Dances with Wolves* and *Thunderheart*. *Imagining Indians* also contains clips of Hopi people vigorously debating whether or not to allow *Dark Wind* to be filmed on Hopi land as well as interviews with Anglo collectors of Indian artifacts.

These Hopi artists are displaying their work in the Santa Fe Indian Market in Santa Fe, New Mexico.

Masayesva, who is from the village of Hotevilla on Third Mesa, studied still photography at Princeton University before he began working with video. He has screened the movie throughout the United States and has edited a sixty-minute version for television. The film is entirely Indian written, produced, filmed, edited, and owned, which makes it a rarity among movies that center on Indians.

From the enjoyment of traditional village life to the production of movies, Hopis have adjusted to many changes in the world while still remaining Hopi.

— D. L. Birchfield

SEE ALSO:

Boarding Schools; Hopi and Navajo Relocation Act; Joint Use Area; Kachina; Masayesva, Victor, Jr.; Navajo; Pueblo; Rose, Wendy; Spain.

SUGGESTED READINGS:

Bonvillain, Nancy. *The Hopi.* New York: Chelsea House, 1994.

Forbes, Jack D. *Apache, Navaho, and Spaniard.* 2nd ed. Norman: University of Oklahoma Press, 1994.

Trimble, Stephen. *The People: Indians of the American Southwest.* Santa Fe: Sar Press, 1993.

HOPI AND NAVAJO RELOCATION ACT

Public Law 93-531, enacted by the United States Congress in 1974, partitioned an area known as the Joint Use Area into two blocks of land, one for the exclusive use of the Hopis, and one for the exclusive use of the Navajos. The land in question had been set aside by executive order in 1882 "for the Moqui [Hopis] and such other Indians as the Secretary of Interior may see fit to settle thereon." Thereafter both Hopis and Navajos had occupied the land. In 1962, a federal court case, *Healing v. Jones,* declared that the Hopis and Navajos were entitled to joint use of the land, and it became known as the Joint Use Area. In dividing the Joint Use Area into exclusive Hopi and Navajo portions, Public Law 93-531, in 1974, required that all Hopis and Navajos who were living in the other tribe's portion of the former Joint Use Area be forced to relocate to new homes. The law affected about one hundred Hopis, who moved from the Navajo portion. However, approximately five thousand Navajos were living on the Hopi portion, and many of them refused to move.

A center of resistance, which developed among many of the Navajo families at Big Mountain, soon attracted media attention. The federal government, hoping to induce the Navajos to relocate voluntarily, offered a five-thousand-dollar relocation bonus for those Navajos who would sign up to move before July 6, 1985. The Navajo tribe also received 400,000 acres (160,000 hectares) of replacement land for displaced Navajo families, but 75,000 acres (30,000 hectares) of that land consists of an abandoned coal mine. By 1994, all but a few hundred Navajos had relocated, but the remaining families refused to leave their homes, which they had been occupying for generations. Federal intermediaries continue to negotiate a settlement between the Hopis and the remaining Navajos.

SEE ALSO:

Hopi; Joint Use Area; Navajo; Navajo Reservation.

HORSES

Horses of half-Andalusian, half-Arabian blood were brought to North America by the Spaniards. In the Southeast, the armored war horses of the de Soto expedition in 1540 struck terror into the hearts of Native people, who had never before seen such animals.

Coronado first brought the horse to the Great Plains grasslands in 1541. Half a century later, the Indians of the Southwest were the first Natives to own horses when the Spaniards colonized New Mexico near the end of the sixteenth century. Plains Indians also acquired their horse herds from the horses of the Spanish in the Southwest. By 1770, horses were widespread in North America.

The horse brought about great changes in Plains Indian cultures. Horses transformed Plains Indians from nomadic peoples, traveling with the change of seasons with the help of dogs and the

This display of traditional dress on horseback was a part of a recent powwow in Connecticut.

travois, into mounted hunters and warriors who could settle in one place but yet remain mobile for the hunt. Some of the most famous Plains Indian tribes did not even live on the Plains before horses became available. The Comanches were originally a Shoshonian people from the Great Basin area, the Sioux were a northern woodlands people living in the forests of the Great Lakes region, and the Crows migrated to the Great Plains from even farther to the east, from the Northeastern Woodlands. The cultures of all of these peoples underwent great changes once they adopted the use of the horse and became buffalo hunters on the Great Plains.

The Comanches and Kiowas of the Southern Plains became large-scale dealers in horses for other Plains tribes. The peak of this trading activity was in the first half of the nineteenth century. By raiding Spanish ranches far into Mexico, the Comanches and Kiowas annually acquired herds of thousands of horses. Periodically, tribes of the Middle Plains, such as the Arapahos, would visit the Comanches and Kiowas and trade for large numbers of horses. They, in turn, would trade many of the horses to the Sioux and other tribes of the Northern Plains.

Indians also became expert horse breeders. Chickasaws and Choctaws bred a specialized horse that became known throughout the South for its stamina and ability to maneuver in close, congested terrain and on steep hillsides. Plains Indians used only the fastest and most intelligent stallions to breed. In time, they molded their original stock to be faster, more intelligent, and more responsive than ever before. The Indian Pintos, Duns, and splotched cayuses were smaller than the white man's heavy, grain-fed horses, and the Indian horse could live off the land, while U.S. Army horses had to have their feed brought with them. In battle or during a buffalo hunt, the Indians' horses were superior. With a horse, a single hunter could kill three or four buffalos, enough to feed an entire family for many months.

Like the dog, the horse was also a beast of burden. Indians of various tribes gave the horse names like Big Dog, Spirit Dog, Holy Dog, and Medicine Dog. By 1910, North America was home to about twenty million domesticated horses.

SEE ALSO:
Coronado Expedition; De Soto Expedition; Dogs.

HOUSE CONCURRENT RESOLUTION 108

On August 1, 1953, House Concurrent Resolution 108 set guidelines for an attempt by the United States to "terminate" its government-to-government relationship with Indian nations. HCR 108 stated that the policy of the United States Congress should be to make Indians subject to the same laws, entitled to the same privileges, and subject to the same responsibilities, as other citizens. Termination would end the status of Indians as wards of the United States and would grant them the rights and privileges pertaining to American citizenship.

Indian nations viewed the resolution as an attempt to break up tribal communities, and as an attempt by the United States to relieve itself of obligations to Indian people which had been secured by treaties. The resolution set forth standards for determining which tribes might be considered candidates for termination. Under those standards, about a dozen Indian nations were cited as prepared for "self-sufficiency." These were nations with a strong economic base and tribal government; therefore, the United States argued that they would be able to maintain self-sufficiency.

Some Indian nations were terminated under HCR 108, until the policy was abandoned by a shift in federal Indian policy in the 1960s. Most of the tribes that were terminated during the 1950s have attempted to regain their status as federally recognized tribes. The Menominees of Wisconsin and the Wyandots of Oklahoma are two tribes that were terminated and have since regained federal recognition.

SEE ALSO:
Federally Recognized Nations and Tribes; Termination Policy.

HOUSER, ALLAN (1914–1994)

Chiricahua Apache sculptor Allan Houser has been acclaimed throughout the world for his six decades of work in wood, marble, stone, and bronze. Houser was born June 30, 1914, near Apache, Oklahoma. He died August 22, 1994, in Santa Fe, New Mexico. His Apache surname was Haozous, which means "Pulling Roots."

Houser was a charter faculty member in the 1960s at the Institute of American Indian Arts in Santa Fe, where he began to cast statues in bronze. He taught until 1975. When he retired from teaching, however, he devoted himself full-time to his work, creating sculptures in bronze, wood, and stone. In April 1994, he presented an 11-foot (3.3-meter) bronze sculpture to first lady Hillary Rodham Clinton in Washington, D.C., as a gift from the American Indians to all people.

Houser was known primarily for his large sculptures. Many of these could be seen in a sculpture garden, arranged among piñon and juniper trees, near his studio. His work is included in the British Royal Collection, the Metropolitan Museum of Art in New York City, the Heard Museum in Phoenix, Arizona, the Denver Art Museum, in Denver, Colorado, the Museum of Northern Arizona in Flagstaff, Arizona, the Linden Museum in Stuttgart, Germany, the Fine Arts Museum of the Museum of New Mexico in Santa Fe, New Mexico, the Apache Tribal Cultural Center in Apache, Oklahoma, the Gilcrease Museum in Tulsa, Oklahoma, and the University Center in Tulsa.

His work won many awards, including, most recently, the Prix de West Award in 1993 for a bronze sculpture titled "Smoke Signals" at the annual National Academy of Western Art show at the National Cowboy Hall of Fame in Oklahoma City, Oklahoma. "Smoke Signals" is now a part of the permanent collection of the National Cowboy Hall of Fame.

One of his best-known works, a bronze statue of an Indian woman titled "As Long as the Waters Flow," stands in front of the state capitol of Oklahoma in Oklahoma City. At the University of Oklahoma in Norman, two large Houser sculptures were on loan to the university and on display on the grounds of the campus at the time of his death. On display at the Fred Jones Jr. Museum on campus were several Houser pieces from private Oklahoma collections. Upon his death, the University of Oklahoma Student Association announced the creation of the Allan Houser Memorial Sculpture Fund. The fund will be used to purchase a major Houser sculpture for permanent display on the University of Oklahoma campus.

Chiricahua Apache sculptor Allan Houser, at work in New Mexico.

The Allan Houser sculpture of Delmar Boni, at the Heard Museum, in Phoenix, Arizona.

HOWARD, OLIVER O. (1830–1909)

One of the principal U.S. Army generals in charge of campaigns during the Indian wars of the late nineteenth century, General Oliver O. Howard is probably best known as the commander of forces that pursued Chief Joseph (The Younger) and his Nez Perce band on their 1,700-mile (2,737-kilometer) Long March in 1877. Howard had originally intended to acquire tribal land by buying out the Nez Perce at a meeting with Joseph and the elderly chief Toohoolhoolzote. But tempers became frayed when the chiefs dismissed Howard's plan out of hand, rejecting the very notion that land could be sold. Toohoolhoolzote spoke with such eloquence and anger that Howard had him locked in the guardhouse. Negotiations ended, and the Nez Perce chiefs agreed reluctantly to move to a reservation at Lapwai, Idaho. On their way to the reservation, the Nez Perce turned north in an attempt to escape to Canada, a flight that is now known as the Long March, with General Howard and four hundred men in pursuit of Joseph, three hundred warriors, and their families.

Before the Long March, Howard was an officer of the Union Army in the U.S. Civil War; he also headed the Freedman's Bureau, which helped educate freed Blacks during the era following the Civil War known as Reconstruction. Howard University, in Washington, D.C., is named in his honor. Howard also persuaded Cochise, the Chiricahua Apache leader, to surrender in 1871 by guaranteeing that his people would remain in Arizona, countermanding earlier directives to march them to Indian Territory in what is now Oklahoma.

Howard wrote of his adversaries with some compassion and humor in his book *Famous Indian Chiefs I Have Known*. A very religious man, he was deeply offended by the behavior of many whites toward Indians. Howard also wrote several books of military history after his retirement from active duty in the army. In addition, he served as superintendent of West Point, the United States Military Academy, between 1880 and 1882.

GEN. OLIVER O. HOWARD.

General Oliver O. Howard pursued Chief Joseph and the Nez Perce in 1877.

SEE ALSO:
Apache; Chief Joseph; Cochise; Nez Perce.

HOWE, LEANNE (1951–)

Native writer Leanne Howe, an Oklahoma Choctaw, was born on April 29, 1951. She is a journalist, poet, short-story writer, playwright, and novelist. As a journalist, she has worked for *The Dallas Morning News* and *USA Today*. She has published two collections of short fiction, *Coyote Papers* and *A Stand Up Reader*. An excerpt from her novel in progress, for which her working title is *The Bone Picker*, was published in 1993 as a short story titled "Danse D'Amour, Danse De Mort," in *Earth Song, Sky Spirit: Short Stories of the Contemporary Native American Experience*, edited by Clifford Trafzer. In 1991, Howe, who reads French, received a grant from the National Endowment for the Humanities to research her novel, which is set in the eighteenth-century Choctaw country in Mississippi and for which she is making extensive use of French historical records. In 1995, she received a fellowship from the McDowell Colony to continue work on the novel.

While living in Texas, Howe coauthored a play, with Choctaw poet Roxy Gordon, titled *Big Pow-wow*, which was produced in Fort Worth, Texas, in 1987 by the Sojourner Truth Players. While living in Iowa, Howe served on a state commission that determines the repatriation of Native American remains. Her play, *Indian Radio Days*, also coauthored with Roxy Gordon, was produced by an Iowa radio station in the fall of 1993, with satellite broadcasts to Native communities in Alaska. During that production, she was interviewed at length by the *Native Playwrights Newsletter*.

Howe is probably best known for her saucy 1989 essay "An American in New York," in *Spider Woman's Granddaughters: Traditional Tales and Contemporary Writing by Native American Women*, edited by Paula Gunn Allen. Her work has appeared in a number of other anthologies, including *Returning the Gift: Poetry and Prose from the First North American Native Writers' Festival*, edited by Joseph Bruchac; *American Indian Literature*, edited by Alan

Choctaw writer Leanne Howe has achieved distinction working in many different creative media.

R. Velie; *Looking Glass*, edited by Clifford Trafzer; and *Reinventing the Enemy's Language*, edited by Joy Harjo. She is also published in journals, including *Studies in American Indian Literatures* and *Fiction International*. Recently, she coproduced her first record album, *Hawk in Hand*, with musician Jarryd Lowder.

HUALAPAI

Hualapai is a corruption of a term meaning "ponderosa pine people" that refers to one of the bands that make up this Yuman-speaking people. Living in northwestern Arizona, the Hualapais were bordered by the Yavapais, Mojaves, and Havasupais. The bands composing the Hualapais can be divided into three subtribes: the Middle Mountain

A Hualapai mother and child bask in the warmth of the sun on the Hualapai Reservation at Peach Springs, Arizona.

People in the far northwest, the Yavapai Fighters to the south, and the Plateau People on the east.

The traditional Hualapais lived primarily by managing the resources of their environment, by gathering seasonal wild plants and hunting. The evidence is uncertain as to whether agriculture was significant for them. Wild mescal, or agave, was a staple food, as were various cactus fruits, piñon nuts, and juniper and sumac berries. They also hunted rabbits, rodents, mule deer, bighorn sheep, and pronghorn antelope. The Hualapais had an extensive trade network, trading not only with their near neighbors, but participating in a larger trade network that encompassed the Pacific Coast Indians and the Pueblos. The Hualapais offered dried mescal, basketry, and hematite, or iron ore, in exchange for other goods.

Other than contact with early explorers, the Hualapais first became aware of non-Indian settlers when the western route going through Needles, California, was built through their territory. Both the Mohaves and Hualapais resisted the intrusion of wagon trains through their territories, which strained the resources of the environment. The U.S. Army led a campaign against the Mohaves and established the Fort Mohave garrison in 1859. After an uneasy peace, the discovery of gold near Prescott, Arizona, brought more Euro-American intrusions into Hualapai country, and relations worsened between settlers and Indians. In 1866, Wauba Yuma, a respected Hualapai leader, was killed by Euro-Americans. In retaliation, the Hualapais gathered a force of 250 men, armed them through their trade network, and fought the U.S. Army throughout the following year. By 1869, Lieutenant Colonel William R. Price finally defeated the Hualapais with superior forces and arms.

Immediately after the conflict, the Hualapais were taken to Camp Beale Springs in 1871 but were moved to the Colorado River Indian Reservation three years later. Conditions there were bad, and the Hualapais escaped to walk back to their traditional territory. Their homecoming found most of their land taken over by cattle ranchers.

At a memorial powwow on the Hualapai Reservation, this Hualapai child and her dog find diversion in the manner of children all over the world.

In 1883, a 900,000-acre (360,000-hectare) reservation was established for the Hualapais. But the land had been changed by heavy cattle grazing, and they were unable to successfully take up their traditional lifestyle again. Many fell victim to the diseases that came with contact with Euro-Americans: smallpox, whooping cough, and syphilis. During this period, the Hualapais embraced the Ghost Dance, introduced by a Paiute in 1889.

Due to the poor quality of the reservation, many Hualapais found jobs in nearby towns on the railroad or in mines and on ranches. In the 1930s, the effects of the Great Depression drove some back to the reservation, where a political structure consisting of a nine-member tribal council was being organized. Economic development on the reservation continued to be virtually nonexistent until the 1970s, however. At that time, the tribal cattle herd was built up, a forestry project was begun, and the Hualapais developed a river raft landing site. Establishment of a doll factory (1973–1980) represented just one of the developing tribal enterprises. Years of Hualapais living off-reservation in order to survive has taken its toll on the cohesiveness of tribal identity and traditional culture, and this continues to be a challenge for the Hualapai tribe.

SEE ALSO:
Arizona; Ghost Dance Religion; Havasupai; Yavapai.

HUDSON'S BAY COMPANY

The Hudson's Bay Company was an English trading company that dominated much of Canada for centuries beginning in 1670. The company was formed when Charles II, king of England, granted a charter to his cousin Prince Rupert and a group of seventeen others. The company monopolized trade in a vast Canadian land area "drained by the waters flowing into Hudson Bay." This area became known as Rupert's Land.

The powerful company built ships of war and forts. It also established laws and carried out punishments for disobeying the laws. Hudson's Bay Company had the authority to work cooperatively with Indians or to make war upon them.

London was the main market for furs and goods coming from the area. By 1749, the enormously successful yearly trade amounted to about four shiploads of British goods for the equal weight of furs and skins. Indians were the main providers of the furs and skins, for which they received muskets, axes, traps, and alcohol.

The monopoly of trade by the Hudson's Bay Company went unchallenged until the late seventeenth and early eighteenth centuries. In 1697, the French temporarily drove the English out of Hudson Bay. But in 1713, in the Treaty of Utrecht, France officially recognized England's claim to the area. Fifty years later, the conquest of Canada by the English opened up the Hudson Bay area for access from the south as well as from the sea. The result was an enormous increase in trade and profits for the Hudson's Bay Company.

Other trading companies and private trappers worked the areas from the Great Lakes up the Saskatchewan River toward the Rocky Mountains. A group of these rivals formed the North West Company in 1783 and began to seriously compete with Hudson's Bay Company. In the early nineteenth century, the two competing companies entered into a trade war. Indians were exploited by both companies; large quantities of alcohol were used to barter with them for thousands of animal skins. Trappers slaughtered the animals during the breeding season, thus endangering the supply of furs for subsequent years.

In 1811, Lord Selkirk, a Scottish philanthropist, purchased land from the Hudson's Bay Company and established the Red River Settlement as a colony for Scottish Highlanders. The land was located on the trade route of the North West Company, which tried to force Lord Selkirk's colonists out of the area. During a conflict in 1816, the local governor and seventeen colonists were killed by men of the North West Company. Lord Selkirk retaliated by taking over the company's western headquarters at Fort William. Court proceedings resulting from the conflict financially ruined both Lord Selkirk and the North West Company.

Because of its greater financial resources and its bay route to Europe, the Hudson's Bay Company became victorious over the North West Company. The two companies merged in 1821 under the Hudson's Bay Company name. By then, its territory stretched all the way to the Arctic Ocean on the north and the Pacific Ocean on the west. But in 1859, the Hudson's Bay Company's trade monopoly was abolished, and trade in the region was opened to everyone.

Beginning in 1870, the Hudson's Bay Company entered into the real estate market, retail trade, and eventually into oil and gas production. In 1970, the company received a Canadian charter and moved its headquarters from England to Canada. To this day, the Hudson's Bay Company is the oldest chartered company in operation in the world.

SEE ALSO:

Beavers; Canada, Native–Non-Native Relations in; North West Company.

HUNT, GEORGE (1854–1933)

George Hunt, a Kwakiutl ethnologist, had a significant impact on the study of the Kwakiutls. He was a major contributor to the work of Franz Boas, the pioneer ethnologist of the Northwest Coast. During his lifetime, Hunt supplied Boas with more than six thousand pages of ethnographic material. He also appeared as coauthor with Boas on *Kwakiutl Tears* (1905) and *Ethnology of the Kwakiutl* (1921).

Born in 1854 at Fort Rupert, British Columbia, Hunt was the son of Robert Hunt, the Scottish broker for the Hudson's Bay Company in British Columbia. Hunt's mother was Mary Ebbetts, a Tlingit or Tsimshian (the historical record is unclear). Hunt was raised in the traditional manner, and had little contact with white immigrants until he was in his twenties. Hunt is first mentioned in Anglo-American history as a guide and interpreter for the Adrian Jacobsen expedition along the North Pacific Coast between 1881 and 1883.

Hunt first met Franz Boas in 1886, after which he assumed a major role in recording Kwakiutl history and customs into English. Boas taught Hunt to write the Native language in a phonetic script that could be precisely translated into English. To support himself while he did scholarly work (which began in earnest about the turn of the century), Hunt worked in canneries and as an expedition guide.

As he became an elder, Hunt also became a political leader among his people. He was one of few Native researchers who maintained the respect of both professional academics and his own people. Hunt also worked as a consultant to the American Museum of Natural History. He died at Fort Rupert.

SEE ALSO:
Hudson's Bay Company.

HUNTING

There were probably six hundred or more tribes in North America at the time of European contact, and hunting played a different role within those tribes. Some tribes depended on agriculture a great deal and only supplemented their diets with hunting. Others depended on hunting to a great extent and followed the great herds that were their primary food source. Between these extremes, one would find that for the majority of tribes, hunting was an important source of food.

Hunters were well regarded in most Indian cultures, and most Indian men were trained to hunt. Hunting helped to form the personalities of most Indian men with its requirements of patience, an

Europeans and non-Native Americans were fascinated by the drama of buffalo hunts on the Great Plains, as depicted in this painting in 1853.

This Navajo man is displaying traditional hunting dress at the Santa Fe Indian Market in Santa Fe, New Mexico.

understanding of nature, and heightened physical and mental abilities and senses. Hunting called for courage and strength and for withstanding difficulties of many types. Most hunters learned to be good trackers and to use camouflage; deer hunters wore deerskins to approach deer.

Early American Indian hunters pursued large game such as mammoths, mastodons, and great bison. These animals stood 12 to 14 feet (3.6 to 4.2 meters) at the shoulder and were very dangerous. After these animals became extinct, Indians favored other large game such as bison and elk. Bear were also hunted, and the grizzly bear terrorized many hunters. Deer, antelope, and wild sheep were also hunted. Finally, there were smaller animals that were hunted for food and for hides. These included the wolf, coyote, fox, wolverine, raccoon, rabbit, weasel, ermine, mink, beaver, marten, badger, skunk, squirrel, chipmunk, gopher, marmot, and porcupine. The last was hunted for its quills. All types of fowl were hunted, and on the Pacific coast, mammals such as the whale, walrus, sea lion, seal, and sea otter were harvested.

Indians relied on many different types of weapons made from stone and wood. Most Indian tribes had individuals who were skilled stone workers and flint knappers, and obsidian and flint were traded over hundreds of miles. From 30,000 B.C.E. until about 500 C.E., the main weapon was the spear or lance. Spears were often launched with an atlatl (a stick with a thong or socket to hold and steady the spear), which resulted in longer and faster flight.

In 500 C.E., bows and arrows began to appear. Bows were made from flexible woods such as ash, yew, or mulberry; composite bows were also made by some tribes with inlays of bone or sinew. Arrows were made from cane or wood and were commonly fitted with turkey, buzzard, hawk, or eagle feathers. A good bowman could hit a moving target at fifty yards (forty-five meters), and there is an account of a Plains Indian who showed off for white soldiers by shooting eight arrows into the air before the first arrow hit the ground. Bows had a good deal of power, as well. At Northern Arizona University, in Flagstaff, there is a buffalo bone on display that has an arrowhead lodged in its inner side; the arrow passed all the way through the buffalo's body to wedge there.

Other weapons were used as well—throwing sticks, bolas, clubs, and even blowguns. In the Southwest, nets were used to trap rabbits. One such net, found in a cave at Black Mesa, Arizona, was 240 feet (73 meters) long and 3 feet (0.91 meters) high. Baited traps and snares were also used.

Hunting was a difficult task. A typical hunting band consisted of about 100 to 150 members. To provide everyone with adequate meat would call for bringing in four deer, two buffalo, or one elk a day. This would, of course, call for constant hunting.

In the 1600s, horses were introduced into much of North America by Spanish explorers. Horses changed Indian hunting dramatically. Before the use of horses, for example, a typical hunting range might consist of 50 miles (80 kilometers); with horses, the range expanded to 500 miles (805 kilometers).

The introduction of firearms in the 1700s and 1800s further altered Indian hunting. With firearms, Indians could more easily hunt game, although their use also resulted in overhunting in some areas.

SEE ALSO:
Guns; Weapons, Native American.

HUPA

The Hupas originally lived along the Trinity River in the Hoopa Valley in northwestern California. At the time of first contact with Europeans, the tribe had about fifteen hundred members. They were living in small villages on mountainous, secluded land.

The Hupas speak an Athabaskan language. Before European contact, they were primarily fishers, hunters, and farmers. They enjoyed an abundance of salmon, sturgeon, deer, elk, panthers, acorns, and tobacco. The Hupas traveled the rivers by dugout canoe and traded their foods for the fish and seaweed that the neighboring Yuroks possessed. Hupas made their own woodworking tools, and homes were made of sturdy cedar planks and beams.

The abundance of food, their good fishing sites, and their oak groves allowed tribal members to accumulate wealth. Their riches were counted in

This design of a cedar plank house of the Hupas of northwestern California is also a style of the Yuroks and Karoks of that region.

dentalium tooth shells, in the red scalps of the pileated woodpecker, in rare furs, and in deer hides. The most valued item was the skin of an albino deer. Riches were accumulated and guarded and then passed from generation to generation. Wealth was passed between families only as a price for a bride, a fee for a healer, or payment of a fine for a wrongdoing.

Many of the tribe's customs were based on wealth. Marriage was by purchase, and the position of tribal chief was determined according to wealth. Wealth was transferred through the male line. Debtors who could not pay their debts and people who could not make payment for their crimes were required to pay with labor.

Ceremonies featured wealth-displaying dances called the White Deerskin Dance and the Jumping Dance. Each of the dances lasted ten days every autumn and were performed by the men. The purpose of the ceremonies was to renew the world, ensure well-being for the community, and deflect illness and bad luck throughout the coming year.

Until 1848, the Hupas lived in isolation and relative peace. They did not like violence and bloodshed. Generally, whenever a problem broke out between individuals or families, a mediator would step in to stop the fighting and to set up payment for any injury, destruction of property, or death. But by 1848, the area was invaded by miners looking for gold, and the Hupas were forced from their homes.

The United States Congress created a Hupa reservation in 1864. Survivors, numbering only a few hundred, live there today. They have tried to maintain their traditions, and today they are well known for their basketry. Farming, livestock raising, and work in the timber and construction industries are important economic activities.

HURON

See Wyandot (Huron).

IDAHO

Idaho became a state on July 3, 1890. The history of Idaho has many connections with American Indians, and there are signs that they may have lived in the area almost fourteen hundred years ago. The first Indians who lived in Idaho were hunters who migrated and who hunted large animals, like mammoths, which are now extinct.

At the time of first European contact in the late 1700s, six major Indian groups lived in the state: In the north lived the Kootenai, the Nez Perce, the Coeur d'Alene, and the Flathead; in the south lived the Shoshone and Bannocks, or Northern Paiutes. These tribes first met Europeans who were fur traders. During 1805 and 1806, the Lewis and Clark expedition traveled through the region, and in 1846, the United States gained control of the Oregon Territory, which included all of present-day Idaho. Permanent white settlement occurred in 1860, when Mormon settlers began to enter the state.

Idaho contains five reservations: The Coeur d'Alene Reservation contains 67,981 acres (27,192 hectares). The Duck Valley Reservation contains 289,819 acres (115,928 hectares). Fort Hall Reservation contains 522,510 acres (209,004 hectares). Kootenai Reservation contains 1,825 acres (730 hectares), and the Nez Perce Reservation contains 85,661 acres (34,264 hectares). The 1990 U.S. Census lists 13,780 Idaho residents as American Indians, making it twenty-ninth among U.S. states in terms of Indian population.

A Shoshone-Bannock man from Idaho displays traditional regalia.

SEE ALSO:
Lewis and Clark Expedition.

IKTOME

Iktome (also spelled *Iktomi*) is a spider trickster who appears in many stories of the Sioux people. Like many other tricksters, Iktome is a rebel against authority, a troublemaker, a player, and a clown.

In addition to being a troublemaker or a clown, trickster can also be a hero, who unwittingly creates a great many useful things during his quest for mischief or revenge. Like the trickster Coyote, Iktome can change his form into anything he desires—as long as he thinks he is getting what he wants. What makes Iktome such a complicated being is that he defies the flesh and blood boundaries of animal or human identity. He is purely contradictory—both wise and stupid, dangerous and clownish, reviled and respected. The trickster is symbolic of all the things in the world that are confusing and contradictory.

Trickster stories are often built upon layers of tricks. When Iktome invents a strategy or a trick to play on some innocent bystander, he often finds that the the trick has turned on himself. Iktome's bag of tricks is sometimes a "house of cards"—that is, one that can easily fall apart or have unintended consequences—and when his scheming ways play him as the fool that he invariably is, a humorous lesson is learned.

Many trickster stories are centered on Iktome's ferocious sexual appetite, like the story "Iktome and the Ignorant Girl," of the Brulé Sioux. Another tale from the Brulé Sioux is "Iktome Sleeps with His Wife by Mistake." In these stories, Iktome becomes the victim of his own trickery.

Storytelling, or the oral tradition, is an immensely rich part of American Indian culture. Stories are passed on from one generation to the next, and most are centuries old. Telling stories may be a way of simply providing entertainment, or they may contain valuable life lessons that teach us how to behave in ways that will ensure a good and worthy life.

One popular story is "Iktome and the Buffalo Skull," summarized here from the Ella Deloria collection: Iktome was out walking one day when he heard singing. Hearing the music made Iktome want to sing and make music, too, but he could not tell where the singing was coming from. He began searching and finally saw that the sound was coming from a buffalo skull lying nearby. He peered through the eye of the skull and saw several mice in the midst of a good time.

It had been a long time since Iktome last enjoyed himself, and he wanted very badly to dance and sing, too. He pushed his head into the skull,

asking the mice if he could join in, whereupon the mice fled in terror at the sight of him. When Iktome tried to remove his head from the skull, he could not. He was stuck and began to panic. He went to a nearby rock and began to beat the skull upon it until it broke apart into many pieces. Iktome had bruised his head badly in the effort, and for a long time afterward, he felt very sick and dizzy.

SEE ALSO:
Coyote Stories; Deloria, Ella; Storytelling; Tricksters.

ILLINOIS

Illinois became a U.S. state in 1818. Illinois's Indian history reaches back thousands of years. Paleo-Indian artifacts dated to 8000 B.C.E. have been found at Modock Rockshelter in the southwestern part of the state. The Archaic Culture, which followed the Paleo-Indian, dates from about 5000 B.C.E., followed by the Woodland and, in southern Illinois, the spectacular Mississippian, which produced the Mound Builders. Two Mound Builder locations, Cahokia Mound and Dickson Mound, are preserved as Illinois historical sites. The Mississippian Culture disappeared before the period of European contact.

When French explorers first entered the region in the late 1600s, the Illinois or Illiniwek tribes were living in the state. Many of the Illinois lived along the Mississippi River and enjoyed the many special resources that the river provided. Under pressure from European settlement and from other tribes that were forced west into the Illinois's territory, the tribe allowed itself to be removed to a reservation in Kansas. Resistance by Indian tribes ended in Illinois with the close of the Black Hawk War in 1832.

No Indian reservations currently exist in Illinois, but the 1990 U.S. Census lists 21,836 Illinois residents as being American Indians. This makes Illinois the twentieth state among U.S. states in terms of Indian population.

SEE ALSO:
Black Hawk; Cahokia; Illinois Confederacy; Mississippian Culture; Mound Builders.

This display of traditional regalia is part of a heritage festival at Cahokia Mounds State Historic Site in Illinois.

ILLINOIS CONFEDERACY

The Illinois Confederacy, after which the state of Illinois is named, was one of the Midwest's largest Native confederations during the 1600s. At this time, European traders first entered their homelands, the present-day states of Iowa, Illinois, and Wisconsin. French sources estimate the population of the confederacy, which included the Cahokia, Peoria, Kaskaskia, Espenimkia, and other nations, at one hundred thousand or more.

In their heyday, the Illinois were a major cultural presence in the Midwest, with a distinguished history. For example, the peoples of this region constructed major cities before contact with Europeans. One of these, called Cahokia, was a major trading center and one of the largest urban areas within the bounds of the area that would eventually become the United States.

Cahokia was a six-square-mile (sixteen-square-kilometer) city containing 120 mounds, as well as thousands of dwellings and places of business. Cahokia served as a center of a trade network reaching from the present-day Dakotas to the Gulf of Mexico, roughly the distance between Paris and Moscow. Evidence indicates that the city at the junction of the Missouri and Mississippi Rivers (near present-day St. Louis) probably housed about thirty thousand people, a size equal to London at the same time, during the thirteenth century.

Cahokia, which included a ceremonial mound larger than any of Egypt's pyramids, was the largest of several population centers that developed in the Mississippi Valley around the year 1000 C.E., possibly influenced through wide-ranging traders by the civilizations of Mesoamerica (Central America). The temple mounds of the Mississippians resembled the constructs of the civilizations to the south, as did their social structure, remnants of which survived into the period of European contact among the Natchez.

By the year 1700, a combination of disease, non-Indian immigration, and attacks by the Iroquois and their allies had reduced the population of the Illinois Confederacy to about sixty-five hundred. The Iroquois completely wiped out the Espenimkia and dealt severe blows to many other tribes of Illinois during the Beaver Wars of the seventeenth century.

The last remnants of the Illinois were scattered after the defeat of the French, with whom they were allied, by the British in 1763. The French had allied with the Illinois because the once-powerful confederacy controlled the Mississippi River between French settlements in the Great Lakes area and Louisiana. During the 1700s, the Illinois (whose name is a French adaptation of their own word for "people") were attacked by several tribes other than the Iroquois. After an Illinois Indian who was paid by the British killed Pontiac in 1769, the wrath of Pontiac's many allies fell upon the Illinois. By the year 1800, the Illinois population was below one thousand. Some of the Illinois eventually migrated to Indian Territory (later Oklahoma), and their descendants live in the northeastern part of Oklahoma today.

SEE ALSO:

Beaver Wars; Cahokia; Central America, Indigenous Peoples of; French and Indian War; Illinois; Iowa, State of; Iroquois Confederacy; Mississippian Culture; Mound Builders; Pontiac; Wisconsin.

INCA

The Incas once had a vast civilization that resided in the present-day South American country of Peru. It was once the wealthiest and most powerful empire in all the Americas. The Incan capital was located in present-day Cuzco, a small city in the Andes Mountains. At its peak, the Inca Empire covered the areas of Peru, Ecuador, Bolivia, and parts of Chile, Colombia, and Argentina. The Inca Empire first began from about 1200 C.E., when the Incas first entered the Andean highlands. Between 1438 and 1532, the civilization flourished as a great empire. The empire collapsed because of disease brought from the outside and civil war conflicts, and eventually it was conquered by the Spanish conquistadores.

The name *Inca* is the Quechua word for "prince" or "male of royal blood." In the days of the Incas, only members of the royal family could be called Incas. Today, any individual belonging to a group once ruled by the Great Inca, or king, is sometimes called an Inca, and the word *Indian* is regarded as an

The ruins of Machu Picchu, the hidden city of the Incas, high in the Andes Mountains, were not discovered until 1911.

These pre-Columbian gold ear ornaments are from the Chimu culture in Peru, one of the many distinguished cultural traditions that flourished before the rise of the civilization of the Incas.

insult in Peru. Natives of Peru prefer to be called *runas* or *indigenas*, and farmers are often referred to as *campesinos*.

There are legends that tell of the birth of the Inca Empire. One story, passed down through generations, tells of Manco Capac, the first Great Inca King, stepping out of a cave in the Cuzco valley one day in the year 1200. Wearing a golden robe and carrying a staff, he pronounced himself king.

Around 1438, a nearby tribe, called the Chancas, threatened to invade the fertile Cuzco valley. The ninth Incan leader by the name of Pachacuti assembled an army to dissuade the Chancas, and he started to construct a fortress to protect the city from invasion. (Archaeological evidence suggests that the city of Cuzco was originally planned to resemble the shape of a puma, one of the animals the Incas regarded as sacred.) Beyond the city, Pachacuti built the fortress called Sacsahuaman, and it is considered the greatest fortress ever built by Native Americans.

The fortress was protected by tall towers and surrounded by enormous walls, some of which are still standing today. Some of the stones in the wall weigh 200 tons (182 metric tons). The fortress is thought to have taken sixty years to build and included underground channels, warriors' barracks, and a maze of streets aboveground.

The Incas also constructed a highly developed road system that wound over the mountainous terrain of the Andes and extended as far as 3,250 miles (5,233 kilometers) across the South American mountains from Ecuador to Argentina. Another road ran along the coast from Peru into Chile for 2,000 miles (3,220 kilometers). The Incas had no wagons or carts, as the wheel was not yet developed; however, the Incas used llamas to carry goods from place to place. Couriers called *chasquis* ran along the roadways, carrying messages and small packages from town to town.

The Incas' vast network of roads connected hundreds of villages and cities. Each city had its own nearby fortress, which resembled the cities

Varieties of corn are sold by an Inca descendant in the Chincheros village market, near Cuzco, Peru, the ancient capital of the Incas. The Incas also developed hundreds of varieties of potato.

The Inti Raymi, Inca Sun Festival, at Sacsayhuaman in Cuzco, "the city of the Sun," is celebrated during the month of June.

themselves. When an enemy threatened, the people relocated to the safety of the fortresses. In proximity to the capital city Cuzco was a stone city called Machu Picchu. Machu Picchu stands hidden some 2,000 feet (606 meters) above the Urubamba River, between two mountain peaks. The city was discovered by Hiram Bingham in 1911. The great city contained terraces for farming, thatched houses, barracks, and temples. The buildings of the Incas were built of carefully cut and polished stone; no cement was used to hold the stones together. Their engineering is a technological marvel. Other Inca cities included Limatambo, Vilcashuaman, Cajamarca, and the recently discovered Vilcapampa, which is thought to be the last stronghold of the defeated Incas and a hiding place the Spanish conquistadores never found.

The majority of the people ruled by the Great Inca were farmers. Many cities had cut terraces resembling steps. These steps provided flat spaces on which to plant, and the stones between the steps kept dirt from washing down during rain. Many types of plants were cultivated, including beans, peanuts, pumpkins, maize (corn), fruits, vegetables, cacao for chocolate, and several different varieties of potatoes. The ancient Peruvians devised a freeze-drying method, making it possible to preserve potatoes for five or six years without spoiling. This type of potato is called *chuno* and is still eaten today in Peru.

The Incas believed in several deities. The most important was Viracocha, the Creator, who was thought to have a human form. Next in rank were the sky gods, which included Inti, god of the sun and founder of the Inca royal lineage, and the gods of thunder, goddesses of the moon, and constellation deities, which were believed to look out for human welfare by guarding plants and animals.

Around 1532, a Spaniard named Francisco Pizarro was instrumental in the collapse of the Inca Empire. He arrived in the cities in search of gold during a time when the Incas were divided in a civil war called the War of Two Brothers. Pizarro killed

This child is carrying a candle in the procession of the Corpus Christi festival at Cuzco in Peru.

the ruler Atahualpa and declared himself governor. In the years that followed, the Spanish seized the Incas' lands, mines, temples, fortresses, and storehouses. The Andean people were forced to work in Spanish homes, fields, and mines. It took the Spanish just a few years to destroy much of the architecture that the Incas had spent years in constructing. So ended the Inca Empire.

Life today for the Inca descendants is very different from their magnificent past. The region that once made up the richest and most powerful empire in the Americas is now among the poorest on earth. Many people live in villages high in the Andes, where the climate is harsh and making a living requires great effort. Many work in mines where conditions are dangerous, and many more are living in towns or cities, hoping to make a better life.

— T. Midge

SEE ALSO:
Central and South Andean Culture Areas; Spain.

SUGGESTED READINGS:
Beck, Barbara L. *The First Book of the Incas*. New York: Franklin Watts, Inc., 1966.
Beals, Carleton. *The Incredible Incas: Yesterday and Today*. New York: Abelard-Schuman, 1973.
Bleeker, Sonia. *The Inca: Indians of the Andes*. New York: William Morrow and Company, 1960.
Metraux, Alfred. *The History of the Incas*. New York: Pantheon Books, 1969.
Newman, Shirlee P. *The Incas*. New York: Franklin Watts, 1992.

INCIDENT AT OGLALA

The stated purpose of the 1991 video documentary *Incident at Oglala* is to show that American Indian Movement (AIM) leader Leonard Peltier did not receive a fair trial when he was convicted of killing two agents of the Federal Bureau of Investigation (FBI) on the Pine Ridge Reservation in South Dakota. Narrated by well-known actor Robert Redford, the documentary is directed by Michael Apted, who also directed the movie *Thunderheart*. That film attempted to present, in dramatic form, the climate of confrontation and violence that existed on the Pine Ridge Reservation in the mid-1970s. Both the movie and the documentary were filmed at the same time and overlap in other ways. For example, John Trudell, who at one time was the national spokesperson for AIM, is interviewed in the documentary and participated in the creation of its sound track, and he is also an actor in *Thunderheart*.

When the seventy-one-day siege of Wounded Knee, South Dakota, ended in May of 1973—and when no network media correspondents remained to tell the world what was happening on the Pine Ridge Reservation—traditional Indians and AIM supporters endured a reign of terror that lasted for more than two years. Frightened by the takeover of the Bureau of Indian Affairs building in Washington, D.C., and by the occupation of Wounded Knee, the mixed-blood leadership of the Oglala Lakota tribal government moved to crush political activism on the reservation while the AIM leadership was tied up in court.

Daily life became life in a police state. Federal authorities allowed—and provided money for—heavily armed vigilantes, called Goon squads (Guardians of the Oglala Nation), who patrolled the roads. The rights to free assembly, free association, and free speech ceased to exist. Violence reigned. Drive-by shootings, cars being run off the road, firebombings, and murders became the norm. During one twelve-month period, there were more murders on the Pine Ridge Reservation than in all the other parts of South Dakota combined; in fact, the reservation had the highest per capita murder rate in the United States. By June 1975, there had been more than sixty unsolved murders of traditional Indians and AIM supporters.

The FBI, charged with solving murders on Indian reservations, took little more than a yawning interest. On June 26, 1975, however, when two FBI agents were killed near the community of Oglala on the reservation, 350 FBI agents were on the scene within three days. But they were not there to find out who had been killing the Indians. *Incident at Oglala* presents the following view of those events.

On June 26, 1975, two FBI agents, new to the area and unknown to its residents, dressed in plain clothes and each driving an unmarked car, reported that they were following a red pickup truck that they believed contained a man who was wanted for stealing a pair of boots. The vehicle actually contained a load of explosives destined for an encampment of about a dozen members of the American Indian Movement not far from Oglala.

For two years, traditional Indians had suffered great losses. Much of the violence had occurred when armed men in vehicles suddenly appeared and started shooting. In this climate of fear and helplessness, with the U.S. government offering no protection, the traditional Indians appealed to AIM for protection. AIM was determined to fight back.

When the two FBI agents followed the red pickup off the road and into a field, a point within earshot of the encampment, a firefight erupted between the agents and the vehicle's occupants, who have never been identified. Armed only with their handguns, the agents attempted to get their rifles out of the trunks of their cars and in doing so exposed themselves to the gunfire.

Hearing the shooting and thinking themselves under attack, men and women from the encampment came running, carrying rifles. They took up positions on a ridge overlooking the vehicles. They were fired at, and they fired back. Bullets filled the air. Within a few minutes, a third FBI agent arrived. This agent had been some fifteen miles (twenty-four kilometers) away and had driven to the scene at more than 100 miles (160 kilometers) an hour. But the first two FBI agents lay dead near their vehicles. The red pickup fled the scene, but not before it had been seen and reported and the report preserved in the records of FBI radio transmissions.

The AIM members up on the ridge went down to the vehicles, where they discovered the bodies of the two FBI agents. Bewildered and frightened, they fled the area on foot under heavy fire, as law enforcement authorities began arriving en masse. An Indian man lay dead. He had been shot through the head at long range. The two FBI agents, already wounded, had been shot through the head at point-blank range.

The full fury of the FBI descended on Pine Ridge Reservation. The director of the FBI appeared on TV and announced a nationwide search for the red pickup.

In the months that followed, the FBI was unable to find the red pickup or its occupants. Three men

who had been at the AIM encampment that day, Darrelle Butler, Bob Robideau, and Leonard Peltier, were arrested and charged with killing the two FBI agents. No one was ever charged with killing the Indian. In Canada, Peltier fought extradition (being handed over) to the United States by the Canadian authorities. In the meantime, Butler and Robideau were tried and acquitted by a jury that believed they had acted in self-defense and that they had not been the ones who executed the wounded agents. The fury of the government then fell on the third defendant, Leonard Peltier.

Documents obtained by perjury and coercion were presented to the Canadian authorities to secure Peltier's extradition. At his trial, the red pickup now became a red and white van, like the one Peltier could be linked to. FBI agents who had filed reports the day of the shooting reporting the red pickup now testified differently, saying their reports had been in error. The government now claimed that the two dead FBI agents—who had reported that they were following a red pickup—did not know the difference between a red pickup and a red and white van.

With the first trial as a blueprint for everything it had done wrong in the courtroom, the government found a sympathetic judge in another jurisdiction. The new judge would make rulings favorable to the prosecution that the first judge had denied and would also make rulings against the defense that the first judge had allowed. The new judge would also not allow testimony about the climate of violence and fear on the reservation, thus effectively thwarting the defense's case of self-defense. By withholding crucial FBI ballistics evidence from the defense and from the court that showed that Peltier's weapon had not fired the fatal shots, the government got a conviction against Peltier. He was sentenced to two life terms in the federal penitentiary.

Incident at Oglala examines the government's case against Peltier and details, step by step, the events of the day the two FBI agents were killed. The documentary presents interviews with the AIM participants, the prosecutors, the defense attorneys, FBI agents, the judge and the jury foreman in the first trial, a U.S. appellate court judge, a U.S. civil rights commissioner, a former governor and a former U.S. senator from South

Dakota, witnesses, and many other people who were involved either in the events at Pine Ridge in those days or in the investigations or the trials. It presents a strong case that Leonard Peltier did not commit the crimes for which he was convicted and that, in a fair trial, he would have been acquitted, as Butler and Robideau were, and argues that the nature of his involvement was the same as theirs.

— D. L. Birchfield

SEE ALSO:
American Indian Movement; Bureau of Indian Affairs; Butler, Darrelle; Peltier, Leonard; Pine Ridge Reservation, Conflict at; Robideau, Robert; Trudell, John; Wounded Knee, Confrontation at (1973).

ADDITIONAL INFORMATION:
Incident at Oglala: The Leonard Peltier Story. Video documentary. Directed by Michael Apted. Narrated by Robert Redford. Music consultants: John Trudell and Jackson Browne. Native American Singing: Quiltman. Carolco International N.V. and Spanish Fork Motion Picture Company, 1991. Live Home Video. 90 minutes.

INDIA

A geographic and spiritual "passage to India" is the image used by Europeans during the Renaissance (roughly the fourteenth through the sixteenth centuries) to romanticize their westward search for "India," an exotic land of spices, jewels, and riches. This impression stimulated the imaginations fed by Marco Polo's journey, the travelogue of Ibn Batuta, and the fictitious *Travells of Sir John Mandeville*, a book supposedly documenting the search for Prester John, a legendary Christian king.

In the fifteenth century, the name India was applied to virtually all of Asia east of Arabia and Persia, including Indonesia, Indochina, China, Japan and all offshore islands, as well as India proper and the modern nations of Pakistan and Bangladesh, which are on the Indian subcontinent and were once part of India proper. And so, when Christopher Columbus sailed west in 1492, he was sure he would reach Catayo (China), Zipangu (Japan), and other parts of what was at the time considered "India."

One of the world's most populous countries, modern India is culturally, linguistically, and reli-

Columbus believed he had sailed to the continent of Asia, or to islands off the coast of India or China. This painting is a romanticized view of his greeting by the people he would soon enslave in the Americas.

giously diverse. Sanskrit, the classic literary language of India, is the language of scriptures, poetry, and historical writing; India's fine arts are among the world's oldest. Land and sea trade with Arab countries brought rare commodities into Italy and Spain, creating a desire in Europe for more of the commodities.

Christopher Columbus and his followers who wanted to explore the Atlantic proceeded west to "India" in order to avoid bandits. The early European explorers had only preconceived notions about "India"; they had no maps and were ignorant of its people. Most scholars feel that Columbus died believing his landfall to be "India" and, in his journals, referred to the *Indies* and the people as *indios*.

The native of India is the only Indian, strictly speaking. The term *American Indian,* which indigenous Americans sometimes reject, is a mutually tolerated misnomer. Immigrants from India proclaim themselves Indo-Americans or Indian-Americans.

Like most immigrants, Asian Indians understand Native Americans according to Hollywood stereotypes, yet they often recognize colonialism as an experience both share. One anecdote describes a Native American attitude about this legacy: While talking with someone from India, a Native elder chuckled, "Columbus got lost looking for you and met us."

SEE ALSO:
American Indians; Columbus, Christopher.

INDIAN ACTIVIST MOVEMENTS

Indian activist movements, which might be defined as Native resistance to the colonization of Indian cultures by European cultures, began with the arrival of the Europeans. During that time, men were warriors within their nations. Today, the warriors are the men and women who fight in the court systems, on the legislative level, and on the community level for the rights of Indian people to maintain their cultures, traditions, and religions.

Some historical Indian activist movements include the Snakes and the Nighthawks. These two groups, Creek and Cherokee, fought against and resisted the allotment of Indian tribal land in Indian Territory in the late nineteenth century. The Ghost Dancers of the late nineteenth century were activists who desired freedom from oppression.

Organized in the late 1960s, the American Indian Movement (AIM) rose to power in the early 1970s. At the same time, an organization known as Indians of All Nations took part in the occupation at Alcatraz Island in California and was joined by AIM members. This demonstration attempted to bring attention to problems faced by Indian people, and it helped spark an era of political activism throughout the continent as Indians reclaimed their pride and organized warrior societies to demand compensation from the United States government for its lack of human rights for Indians. In the spring of 1973, members of the American Indian Movement took over the small town of Wounded Knee on the Pine Ridge Reservation in South Dakota. The seventy-one-day standoff with the United States military brought national media attention to Indian problems.

With the government's constant attacks on AIM members, the organization began to splinter in the mid-1970s, but the pride and struggle continued. From the American Indian Movement other groups formed, including a diplomatic arm of AIM called the International Indian Treaty Council. Another organization to form during that era is the Women of All Red Nations.

Today, there are activist movements within virtually every Indian community in the United States. The movements call attention to human rights violations against Indians and attempt to maintain Indian treaty rights.

SEE ALSO:
Alcatraz, Occupation of (1969); American Indian Movement; General Allotment Act; Ghost Dance Religion; Indian Defense League of America; Oklahoma; Resistance, Indian; Wounded Knee, Confrontation at (1973).

INDIAN ALCOHOL AND SUBSTANCE ABUSE PREVENTION

SEE Alcoholism.

In August 1946, President Harry Truman signed the bill that created the Indian Claims Commission.

INDIAN CLAIMS COMMISSION ACT

The Indian Claims Commission Act was signed by President Harry S. Truman on August 15, 1946. The primary purpose of the act was to restructure the process by which Native people pursued claims to Indian land that had been given up to the United States over the history of dealings between the government and Indian peoples. In many cases, the government had gotten Indians to cede Indian lands through fraud, coercion, misrepresentation of facts, and other questionable means. The Indian Claims Commission Act would provide new avenues to justice for Native people and groups who felt that Indian lands had been unfairly or illegally ceded.

Since 1881 and up to the passage of this act, the process of pressing claims against the government had proven cumbersome and unfair. The United States Congress was required to vote on each individual case before it went to court, and the Court of Claims, where the cases were heard, often introduced biases against the Natives into the processing of the cases. The court's authority did not always extend to all of the tribal claims, and of the two hundred claims filed by 1946, only twenty-nine received awards, and the rest were dismissed on technicalities.

Congress began considering the idea of restructuring in the 1930s, and by the 1940s, leaders of both the Democratic and the Republican parties agreed that something had to be done as claims cases continued to mount against the government. The act of 1946 created a judicial body exclusively to hear the Indian claims against the government, and it allowed the claims to cover more grievances against the government. It also established a date that would close all filings of claims.

The act did not assure the success of claims against the government. The Indian nations had to hire their own attorneys, who had to have the approval of the secretary of the Interior, while the attorney general represented the United States government. The tribes also paid the expenses of litigations, attorney fees included.

The claims commission was originally composed of three commissioners but was expanded to five members in 1967. Only one of the eleven commissioners who served on the commission was Indian. Brantley Blue, a Lumbee, was appointed by President Richard Nixon in 1969.

If the claims commission found the United States liable, it authorized awards, in the form of money, to the Indian nations. The award money was determined by the market value of the land when it was first taken by the government. The commission was not able to restore or return the land to the Indians. With the tribes hiring their own attorneys and paying for litigation, many had to borrow money from the Bureau of Indian Affairs Revolving Loan Fund and pay the money back after the tribes were granted an award. The award money was placed in the U.S. Treasury until Congress directed its distribution among the tribal members. The secretary of the Interior had to approve the decisions by the tribes for the distribution of their money.

Many of the lawmakers who helped pass the Indian Claims Commission Act hoped that such an act would settle long-outstanding claims against the government and thus terminate the government's trust and treaty obligations with the tribes. This would effectively put an end to much of the federal government's historic obligations to Indian peoples. The passage of the act did not terminate these obligations, however, although the government has repeatedly tried to terminate its obligations since.

By the mid-1990s, the commission had worked with six hundred claims that covered a period of about 150 years. It had completed 342 cases and awarded about $818 million to tribes for land taken by government misconduct. It had transferred over sixty cases to the Court of Claims. Even though the government was pleased with the results, many of the Indian nations were not. The Sioux and the Western Shoshones, for example, have had sometimes volatile disputes with U.S. agencies concerning their claims to land.

Many among the Sioux have refused to accept money for the Black Hills, because the Black Hills are sacred to them and cannot be replaced with money. Meanwhile, the Western Shoshones have had heated confrontations with government agencies concerning grazing rights on Western Shoshone land, in accordance with the Treaty of Ruby Valley. Even though some of the claims have been settled, the Indians were not paid the value of the land in current terms and many land issues remain unresolved.

SEE ALSO:
Black Hills; Dann Sisters; Sacred Sites; Termination Policy.

INDIAN COUNTRY

Indian tribal territory has held a distinct status under federal law. The term *Indian Country* describes lands set aside for the use of Indians. Within Indian Country, tribes exercise significant government powers and have important economic and property rights. Once lands are designated as Indian Country, the land status does not change unless Congress takes specific action to do so.

The term *Indian Country* was first used in the eighteenth century during the period when the government's approach to Indian policy was to set aside land for Indians and keep them separate from non-Native settlers. The term was used in early trade acts regulating Indian affairs but, at that time, never formally defined by lawmakers. The context of the trade acts suggested that the term applied to land owned and occupied by tribes. The Nonintercourse Act of 1834 described certain lands west of the Mississippi River as being Indian Country, but that definition was deleted in 1874 during statute revisions when it was no longer suitable because of the United States' continuing expansion west.

Indian Country defines not only a particular geographic area, but also the area where tribal and federal law apply and state law does not, unless specifically excepted by Congress. The Supreme Court has ruled, for example, that tribal members living within reservation boundaries are not under state tax jurisdiction unless authorized by Congress. This principle has been upheld in cases concerning personal property taxes, taxes on receipts from sales, hunting license fees, and other taxes. Outside of Indian Country, tribal members are subject to the same state laws as other state citizens.

In 1948, Indian Country was defined in the United States Code as all land within the boundary of an Indian reservation and under the jurisdiction of the United States. The definition includes dependent Indian communities such as the New Mexico pueblos where Indians occupy lands never officially designated as reservation land.

Indian Country has become a term widely known and widely used by Native media. *News from Indian Country* and *Indian Country Today* are two newspapers that cover events of importance to Indian Country across the North American continent.

The definition also includes all Indian allotments where the title to the land remains in Indian hands. Allotments are parcels of reservation land that were given to individual Indians under the General Allotment Act. The Supreme Court has held that Indian Country includes trust allotments within former reservation boundaries even where no formal reservation currently exists. Although the term is included as part of a criminal statute, the Supreme Court has held that it applies in civil matters as well.

The term *Indian Country* encompasses approximately three hundred federal Indian reservations and more than fifty-two million acres (twenty-one million hectares) of Indian land. This includes not only land held in trust, where the United States government holds the land title on behalf of a tribe, but also allotments owned by non-Indians and located within the boundaries of an Indian reservation. Today, in certain circumstances, tribes can acquire land in trust that enjoys the benefits of Indian Country, a valuable consideration for tribal economic development. This includes land taken in trust under the Indian Reorganization Act (also known as the Indian New Deal) and the Indian Gaming Regulatory Act.

SEE ALSO:

General Allotment Act; Indian Gaming Regulatory Act of 1988; Indian New Deal (Indian Reorganization Act); Indian Trade and Intercourse Acts.

INDIAN DEFENSE LEAGUE OF AMERICA

During the 1920s, the Indian Defense League of America began to protest the violation of treaty rights, particularly among eastern tribes. The Defense League was organized by Clinton Rickard, a Tuscarora chief, and David Hill, a Mohawk from the Six Nations reserve at Brantford, Ontario.

The Defense League was begun as an agency to provide legal representation for Indian people who were too poor to afford it. Protesting Native people refused to pay customs duties or to surrender passports at the United States–Canadian border, because they believed both actions to be violations of the Jay Treaty (in the United States) and the Treaty of Ghent (in Canada). The Indians' position was upheld in court decades later, after similar protests in the late 1960s.

Shortly after 1920, a wave of sympathy emerged in response to the cruelties imposed on Native people during the reservation era. This wave of political opinion produced the *Meriam Report* (1928), which documented the horrid condition of human health and welfare under the "wardship" of the Bureau of Indian Affairs (BIA).

The actions of Indians in the Defense League was complemented by those of non-Indians. By 1923, an organized committee of influential Indians and non-Indians, the Committee of One Hundred, was lobbying for more respectful and humane treatment of surviving American Indians. John Collier was an early member, with lawyer and politician William Jennings Bryan, Clark Wissler, General John J. Pershing, presidential political adviser Bernard Baruch, newspaper editor William Allen White, and the Iroquois Arthur C. Parker. Parker was elected presiding officer at a convention in Washington, D.C., during December 1923. Under his leadership, in 1924, the group published its findings under the title *The Indian Problem*. This document formed the basis for the better-known *Meriam Report* four years later.

The activities of the Defense League, which continued through the 1950s, especially the activities of Wallace Anderson, were the forerunners of Native American activism in the 1960s, which gained national media attention with the occupation of Wounded Knee in 1973.

SEE ALSO:

Anderson, Wallace; American Indian Movement; Collier, John; Indian New Deal (Indian Reorganization Act).

INDIAN GAMING REGULATORY ACT OF 1988

During the 1980s, several reservation Indian nations began operating high-stakes bingo operations and casinos as a source of income for running their services and social programs and as a way of providing jobs to tribal citizens. In several states where casinos were beginning to prosper, non-Native politicians began to question the sover-

Wallace Anderson, right, shown in a theatrical production, was a prominent leader of the Indian Defense League of America.

701

Issues regarding Indian gaming and the establishment of casinos like the one shown here have produced legislation and court cases that uphold powers of tribal sovereignty.

eignty of Indian nations and tried to make the nations comply with state laws and regulations concerning gambling.

In southern California, for example, the Cabazon tribe won court cases against state and county governments that had tried to shut down the tribe's gambling casino. Eventually, the United States Supreme Court was asked to rule in the case, and in 1987, the court upheld the lower court decisions giving the tribe the right to operate its casino.

Lawmakers from other states continued the effort to close or restrict the operation of Indian gaming casinos, however, and in 1988, Congress passed the Indian Gaming Regulatory Act. This act strengthened the Bureau of Indian Affairs' responsibility to oversee Indian gaming. It also established the National Indian Gaming Commission within the Department of the Interior. This commission has the authority to create rules and regulations for Indian gaming.

The act created three classes of gaming. Class I is for social gaming with prizes of low monetary value or for traditional forms of Indian gaming associated with ceremonies and celebrations; Class II gaming includes bingo and similar games; and Class III covers gaming involving pari-mutuel betting, such as dog and horse racing, and casino games. According to the Indian Gaming Regulatory Act, a tribe may conduct Classes II and III gaming in states that allow similar forms of gambling for non-Indians. In states where the state does not allow similar types of gaming, the law also allows the tribes to negotiate with the states for exemption from state laws on gambling.

The gaming commission regulates Class II gaming with the tribes, but Class III gaming requires a compact between a tribe and a state. This law made creating a gaming facility more difficult for the tribes because compacts with the state must be negotiated to the satisfaction of not only both parties but the Department of the Interior, as well.

In 1992, new laws came into effect forbidding Indian casinos from operating electronic slot machines or keno without state approval. The gaming arguments have continued well past the mid-1990s. In response to the success of Indian gaming operations, some states have hurried to pass gaming regulations for non-Indians so that the states may create Class III gaming facilities before Indian groups have a chance to establish them.

SEE ALSO:
Gaming.

INDIAN GIVER

The term *Indian giver* is a colloquial expression that has been used throughout the 1800s and 1900s, meaning to take back a gift previously given. The term has quite negative connotations and is regarded as offensive. Many liken the term to other negative colloquial expressions such as *honest Injun* and *Indian summer*. Honest Injun was originally meant sarcastically, meaning that the person was lying; and Indian summer, despite the positive impression it gives of a warm spell during an otherwise cool autumn, is a term whose origins suggest a false summer. There are nearly five hundred terms that begin with the word *Indian;* many unfairly attack the honesty or intelligence of American Indians.

The origins of both the term and the idea of an *Indian giver* are difficult to determine. In colonial times, an Indian giver was one who expected a present in return. And there is other evidence to suggest that whites observed American Indians taking back their gifts when they didn't get equally valuable ones in return. The Smithsonian Institute's 1901 *Handbook of the American Indians* defines the practice as an "alleged custom," which suggests that non-Indians who observed Indians supposedly taking back gifts may have neither fully understood nor adequately investigated what they were reporting. It may be, too, that the practice of taking back gifts has historically been widely exaggerated by non-Indians who failed to understand the custom of letting others keep an object of value for a while with the expectation that the object would at some time be returned.

It is also possible that the expression is explained by the fact that the term *Indian* was once widely used as a synonym for bogus or false.

To many who have studied the history of Indians after contact with Europeans and European-Americans, the term is also ironic. So many promises were made to Indians by the government and so many promises taken back that to many, the term is more appropriate when applied to the government that revoked countless treaties with the Indians.

INDIAN HEALTH SERVICE

The Indian Health program became a primary responsibility of the U.S. Public Health Service under an act passed on August 5, 1954. Indian Health Service falls under the Department of Health and Human Services.

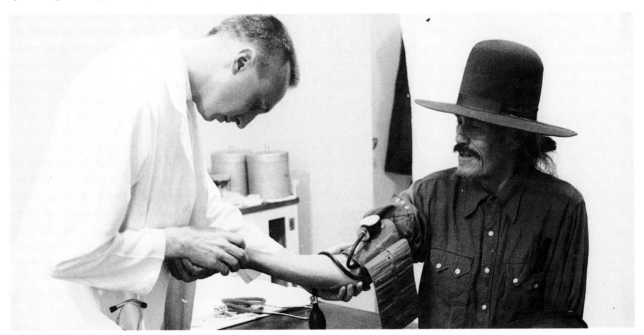

A Navajo man receives treatment at the outpatient clinic of the Public Health Service Indian Hospital at Fort Defiance, Arizona.

From deplorable Indian health facilities only a short time ago, many facilities today offer good health care, but there are not enough of them for the populations they attempt to serve.

The Transfer Act of 1954 states that all functions, responsibilities, authorities, and duties relating to maintaining and operating hospital and health facilities for Indians and conserving Indian health are to be administered by the surgeon general of the United States Public Health Service.

The goal of the Indian Health Service (IHS) is to raise the health status of American Indians and Alaska Natives. Its mission is to provide a health services delivery system with the opportunity for tribal involvement in developing and managing programs to meet their health needs. IHS develops and operates health facilities to provide preventive, curative, rehabilitative, and environmental services to Indian people.

The Indian Self-Determination Act of 1975 gives Indian nations the option of staffing and managing IHS programs in their communities. In 1976, the Indian Health Care Improvement Act was passed with the intention of raising the health status of Indians and Alaska Natives to a level equal to that of the general population through a larger IHS budget. The funding was used to expand services, build and renovate facilities, and construct safe drinking water and sanitation facilities. It also established programs to increase the number of Indi-

an health professionals and to improve health care access for Indians living in urban areas.

In 1993, there were 143 administrative units, called service units, 70 of which were operated by Indian nations. IHS operated 41 hospitals, 66 health centers, 4 school health centers, and 44 health stations. Indian nations operated 8 hospitals, 110 health centers, 4 school health centers, 62 health stations, and 171 Alaska village clinics.

In 1993, over one million people visited IHS facilities. Because of the numbers of IHS users and the lack of funding for staff, IHS users often find themselves sitting in long lines waiting for care. And once in for care, IHS users may find they have little time with their doctors. Despite the advantages of IHS facilities and programs, many services cannot be offered because of lack of funding.

The greatest concentration of services is for pregnant women and for children.

INDIAN MAJOR CRIMES ACT

The Indian Major Crimes Act, passed in 1885, made the federal government responsible for investigating, prosecuting, and punishing specific felonies committed on Indian reservations, thereby taking responsibility away from the Indian nations on whose reservations the crimes had been committed. The felonies for which the federal government now has jurisdiction include murder, rape, assault, larceny, burglary, fraud, and embezzlement.

One incident that probably directly influenced the passage of the Major Crimes Act involved the assassination of one Brulé Sioux leader by another. On August 5, 1881, Crow Dog, who was angry over a tribal leadership dispute, assassinated Spotted Tail by shooting him as he rode along a trail on the Rosebud Reservation in present-day South Dakota. Another Brulé leader arrested Crow Dog two days later and took him to Fort Niobara. Black Crow, who was thought to be a conspirator in the killing, was also arrested. The Brulés handled the matter in a traditional way, settling the case by a tribal council meeting that, following Brulé law, ordered peacemakers sent to both Crow Dog's and Spotted Tail's families. Crow Dog's family paid six hundred dollars, eight horses, and one blanket to the family of Spotted Tail, and harmony was restored within the Brulé tribe. However, a year later, Crow Dog was tried in the Dakota territorial court, convicted of murder, and sentenced to death.

Crow Dog's case was appealed, and his conviction was overturned in a landmark U.S. Supreme Court decision that ruled that the federal courts had no jurisdiction over crimes committed on reservation treaty lands. Thus, it was recognized that American Indians had sovereignty and were entitled to uphold their own laws. But in 1885, largely in response to the Crow Dog case, Congress passed the Major Crimes Act, which provided that an Indian who committed any of a specific number of "major" crimes against another Indian, such as murder or burglary, was subject to the laws of the territory or state in which the crime was committed. And so, Crow Dog's case played a key role in the expansion of federal jurisdiction over events occurring on Indian land.

Following passage of the Major Crimes Act, in which the federal government felt it would show Indians the "majesty of civilized law" over the above-mentioned major crimes, the government also tried to extend its power over minor crimes. As part of its effort to extend its presence into Indian reserva-

tions, the government created tribal police forces, trained by federal government agencies and the Bureau of Indian Affairs police. While members of these tribal forces were certainly better known to members of the Native community, many were also willing to ignore traditional beliefs and tribal sovereignty in order to gain personal standing and prestige in the dominant non-Native society.

Many of these Indian "police" actually played the role of scouts for the U.S. military. For a price, scouts might help the army locate "stray" bands of Indians, whereupon the wanted Indians would be taken prisoner and, in many cases, executed by the army.

Often the "major crimes" that led the scouts and U.S. Army to track certain bands of Indians included such offenses as raiding cattle. Reservation Indians had almost no game to hunt and were given sparing rations, so they often were hungry and raided nearby ranches for food. They also raided government stores where their rations were kept.

With the movement to recognize tribal sovereignty and control that has been a matter of federal policy since the 1970s, Indian nations have taken more authority on investigating crimes. Yet critics of the Major Crimes Act point out that the act still has a grip on Indian nations, creating a disadvantage for Indian people in that most crimes committed on Indian land are committed by Indian people. With federal jurisdiction, Indians are tried in federal courts and punished in federal prisons. And federal courts are more likely to produce tougher sentences than are local and state courts.

SEE ALSO:

Crow Dog; *Incident at Oglala*; Indian Policy, U.S.; Self-determination; Spotted Tail; Wounded Knee, Confrontation at (1973).

INDIAN MEDICINES

As early as 1635, after less than a generation in North America, English colonists were using herbal medicines introduced to them by the Native peoples. *A Relation of Maryland*, written to give prospective immigrants information on the new colony, included this passage: "This Countrey affords

Like this Seminole woman, many Native people continue to draw upon the generations of knowledge of the medicinal properties of plants possessed by traditional Native physicians.

naturally, many excellent things for Physicke and Surgery, the perfect use of which, the English cannot yet learne from the Natives: They have a roote which is an excellent preservative against Pyson [poison], called by the English the Snake roote. Other herbes and rootes they have wherewith they cure all manners of wounds; also Saxafras, Gummes, and Balsum. An Indian seeing one of the English, much troubled with the tooth-ake, fetched of the roote of a tree, and gave the party some of it to hold in his mouth, and it eased the pain presently."

Captain John Smith learned through Pocahontas that her people applied a root she called *wighsacan* to wounds for its healing power. John Lawson, visiting the Carolinas about 1700, observed that Native people there chewed a root (which he did not name) to soothe stomach ailments. European observers also wrote of Indians who committed suicide by eating certain roots and mushrooms. William Penn wrote that a Delaware woman who had been betrayed by her husband "went out, plunk't a Root out of the Ground, and ate it, upon which she immediately died." Native peoples often warned Europeans which plants would make them ill, produce skin rashes, or kill them if eaten. In

some cases, they also provided antidotes. The Delawares, for example, dealt with the rash produced by contact with poison sumac by preparing a tea from the inner bark of the sour gum tree, which gave off a distinctive odor that caused Native peoples to compare it to raw fish.

Most Native American peoples used the byproducts of animals, as well as plants, for medicinal and cosmetic purposes. English immigrants in Virginia and Massachusetts learned early that bear grease allowed Native people to range in the woods wearing a minimum of clothing on hot summer days without being bitten by mosquitoes and other stinging insects. Goose grease and bear fat were widely used as hair dressings, and skunk oil was sometimes applied to the chest and throat to relieve the symptoms of colds, including chest congestion. The Delawares sometimes slowed the flow of blood from a cut by inserting spider webs, which probably helped with blood clotting.

By the eighteenth century, Euro-American observers, many of them missionaries, were compiling lists of Native herbal remedies, some of which were published in several European languages. Peter

Kalm, the Swedish botanist, visited the Middle Atlantic states between 1748 and 1750 to catalogue Native medicinal herbs. One list carried to Europe the knowledge that the bark of a particular tree that grows in North America could alleviate toothache and that the Canadian shrubby elder could be used to combat aches and inflammations. The berry of the wintergreen would calm the stomach. The jalap root could be used as a laxative and to relieve the pain of rheumatism; the Ipecacaunha also functioned as an emetic (which would cause vomiting in case of poisoning), as well as an antidote to snakebite.

Some Native plant remedies worked biologically, while others took Europe by storm on the basis of claims alone. Use of sassafras root (the "Saxafras" in the *Relation of Maryland*, above) was noted as early as Shakespeare's time. The use of sassafras tea spread throughout Europe as a general health tonic, and a trading network grew up across the Atlantic specializing in its harvest, sale, and shipping. At about the same time, all sorts of extravagant claims were being made for the tonic effects of tobacco that do not stand up to scientific scrutiny. Tobacco was said to aid digestion, cure toothaches, kill nits and lice, and even stop coughing. The advocates of tobacco seemed to draw their advice from Native peoples who often used tobacco as a ceremonial herb and rarely became addicted to the use of nicotine.

One student of Native American natural medicines has written that 88 plants were used against colds, 113 to reduce fever, 191 to treat wounds, 41 to calm the nerves, 68 as laxatives, and more than 100 as remedies for stomach pain. Another study cataloged 84 botanical medicines used by mixed-blood Rappahannocks living in the Tidewater region of Virginia, then compared them to lists of established remedies. Sixty percent of the Native remedies had proven medicinal value.

By the late twentieth century, more than two hundred drugs first used by American Indians were listed in the United States *Pharmacopoeia*. These included quinine, laxatives, muscle relaxants, and nasal remedies, as well as several dozen drugs and herbal medicines.

Witch hazel is an example of a Native botanical remedy that has been adopted generally by Euro-American society. Used as a first-aid treatment for

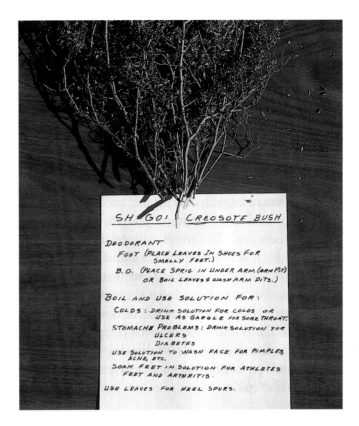

Pimas have found many medicinal and cosmetic uses for the creosote bush.

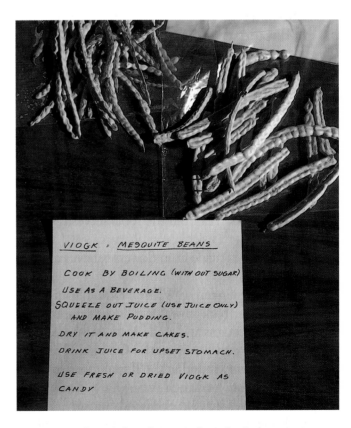

Pimas have found that the juice from boiled mesquite beans is an effective treatment for upset stomach.

U.S. government housing at Zuni Pueblo, New Mexico. Most Indian nations now run the U.S. government housing program for their people as a part of their tribal government, thus providing much-needed administrative jobs for Indian people.

that the European-American lifestyle was superior to that of the Native American and that Native cultures were doomed to extinction.

A critical problem throughout the history of U.S. Indian policy lay in defining the status of the Native American in regard to the United States government. Native Americans were not quite U.S. citizens and not quite inhabitants of independent nations; they became a part of the nation yet remained sovereign in some ways.

When the Europeans colonized North America, they conducted their policy with Native people through treaty making. The fledgling United States government continued the policy of treaty making from 1778 through 1876. Many of the treaties made during this period continue to be in effect today. During this early period, Native Americans were treated as foreign dependent nations, and thus the federal government, rather than the individual states, was responsible for dealing with them. The Continental Congress established a Committee on Indian Affairs to guide Indian policy. This changed in 1786, when Secretary of War

Henry Knox was given responsibility for Indian affairs. The goals of the policymakers were simple: to obtain land from the Native Americans, to establish trading partnerships, and to maintain friendly relationships with them.

Members of the early U.S. government were interested in maintaining a good relationship with their Native neighbors as they represented a formidable force to the new nation. However, the federal government treaty structure was no match for the greed of its citizens, who continually violated established agreements and intruded on Native lands.

Knox initiated some important doctrines in his new position, as hostilities between Indians and European-Americans increased. He proposed that treaties not be based on land acquisition through "right of conquest," but on purchase and compensation for all lands acquired from the Indians. He further recommended that unruly Euro-Americans be prevented from encroaching on lands occupied by Native Americans. As a result, a series of laws called the "Indian Trade and Intercourse Acts" were established between 1790 and 1834. Among other things, they prohibited settlement on Indian lands by non-Indian settlers and established government trading houses with the Indians. An important concept that arose because of these laws was that of "Indian Country," lands outside the boundaries of the United States that fell under federal legal jurisdiction.

In 1819, Congress appropriated funds for the education and "civilization" of Native Americans. These funds were given to various missionary societies. Thus, education became a religious charge rather than a secular, or nonreligious, one. In spite of these efforts by the federal government, the relationship between Native Americans and European-Americans continued to be primarily a hostile one, chiefly because of the illegal sale of liquor to Indians and the illegal seizure of Indian lands by white settlers.

In 1824, the Indian Office, later called the Office of Indian Affairs, was created within the War Department to bring Indian matters under a single central authority. In 1832, the office of commissioner of Indian Affairs was established to provide leadership to the Indian Affairs Office, which later became known as the Bureau of Indian Affairs. In 1849, the Bureau of Indian Affairs was transferred to the new Department of the Interior from the Department of War. This agency, which was staffed initially through political patronage, evolved into the civil service bureaucracy that would carry out U.S. Indian policy.

The treaty and trade policies gave way to the concept of removal after the United States made the Louisiana Purchase. The policy to remove and isolate Native Americans from the European-Americans emerged in the early 1800s. Most Euro-Americans viewed the western land as a remote place that the Indians could be sent to live, far beyond the settled areas on the East Coast. Emigration to "Indian Country" was encouraged, but voluntary, until Andrew Jackson became president of the United States. His administration has become synonymous with the policy of forced Indian removal, characterized by such brutal examples as the Cherokees' Trail of Tears march to Oklahoma under armed guard from their homelands in the Carolinas and Georgia. These actions ignored the landmark Supreme Court case in 1831 that redefined the status of Native American tribes as "dependent domestic nations."

As the western frontier broke down under the unending westward migration of the European-Americans, U.S. policy changed again. It became clear that the concept of removal of all Native Americans to a far western "Indian Country" was not possible after the acquisition of all land between the two coasts. The government's ability to control the intrusion of its citizens into Indian Country was nonexistent. State after state petitioned for entry into the United States, leaving no "Indian Territory."

Beginning in the 1850s, the reservation policy took hold. Native Americans were concentrated onto small areas of land, usually somewhere within the vast area they originally occupied. This new policy represented a change to the previous removal policy of concentration and isolation. If Native Americans strayed from the reservations, they were considered to be "at war" and were subject to attack by the U.S. Army. The reservation policy period was marked by fierce hostilities on the western frontiers, as Native Americans attempted to defend their traditional territories against the ever-encroaching European-Americans.

Aware of the enormous drawbacks of existing Indian policy, reformers clamored for changes. The former philosophy of concentration and isolation of Native Americans yielded to a new philosophy—that of education and assimilation. The new thought was that Native people could be educated to participate fully in the dominant society. The 1870s saw the beginnings of a governmental education program for the Indians, based on a boarding school model and an end of treaty making.

In 1887, the passage of the Allotment Act, or Dawes Act, signaled another new Indian policy—that of allotment. This law allowed the United States to break up reservation lands into individual holdings, or allotments, for all tribal members and promoted the underlying policy of assimilation. Allotment had devastating implications for the continued cultural identity of the tribes. Native Americans were used to holding land in common, not individually. As long as tribal lands were held in common by the tribe, they generally were not relinquished legally or willingly to non-Indians. Once common land was broken up into small

This Indian Peaks Reservation land was lost by the Paiutes in Utah under the federal government's program of "termination" of Indian nations.

parcels and given to the tribal members as individual landholders, they became subject to corrupt land-grabbing schemes.

In 1924, citizenship was conferred upon all Native Americans. John Collier took office as commissioner of Indian Affairs in 1933 and encouraged substantial changes to national Indian policy. The Indian Reorganization Act of 1934 was passed, which attempted to establish self-government for the Indian tribes. The Dawes Allotment Act was repealed, and the Indian Claims Commission was established to hold hearings and restore properties to Indian tribes. Within two years, it restored more than two million acres (eight hundred thousand hectares) of land that had been either illegally or unethically taken from Indian tribes. In the educational arena, Collier promoted community-based schooling instead of boarding schools.

All of these events brought about another change in policy. The government began again dealing with American Indians as nations, not as individuals, as it had under the previous allotment policy. However, an underlying policy of assimilation into the dominant society persisted throughout this change.

The 1948 Hoover Commission report repeated that assimilation of Native Americans was the official public policy of the United States. A new policy of voluntary relocation and termination dealt with both tribes and individuals in the post-World War II era. Voluntary relocation refers to the postwar program of job training and relocation to the cities offered to those individuals wishing to move off the reservation.

From 1953 to 1958, Congress voted to terminate relationships with several tribes. Termination meant that the tribes were no longer under the administration of the Bureau of Indian Affairs but were on their own. All federal benefits were cut, and tribes were advised to apply to the state for benefits. This resulted in enormous hardship on members of some of the terminated tribes who were not prepared with the tools or knowledge necessary to operate their own government and care for all of their people.

President Richard Nixon's 1970 message to Congress outlined a policy of self-determination for Native Americans. Instead of withdrawing all federal assistance programs, as under the previous era's termination policy, Native American tribes would be invited to provide leadership for federal Indian programs. Under a policy of self-determination, federal assistance in the form of tribal economic development programs has been fundamental. Notably, this policy was not designed to promote assimilation into the majority culture but may be used to conserve and promote Native American tribal culture and identity.

— M. A. Stout

SEE ALSO:
Bureau of Indian Affairs; Collier, John; General Allotment Act; Indian Claims Commission Act; Indian Country; Indian New Deal (Indian Reorganization Act); Indian Trade and Intercourse Acts; Jackson, Andrew; Relocation Program; Removal Act, Indian; Self-determination; Self-determination Policy; Termination Policy; Trail of Tears.

SUGGESTED READINGS:

Fixico, Donald L. *Termination and Relocation: Federal Indian Policy, 1945–1960.* Albuquerque: University of New Mexico Press, 1986.

Prucha, Francis Paul. *American Indian Policy in the Formative Years: The Indian Trade and Intercourse Acts, 1790–1834.* Lincoln: University of Nebraska Press, 1970.

Tyler, S. Lyman. *A History of Indian Policy.* Washington, D.C.: Bureau of Indian Affairs, 1973.

INDIAN REMOVAL ACT

SEE Removal Act, Indian.

INDIAN REORGANIZATION ACT OF 1934

SEE Indian New Deal (Indian Reorganization Act).

INDIAN RODEO ASSOCIATION

SEE Rodeos, Indian.

INDIAN SELF-DETERMINATION AND EDUCATION ASSISTANCE ACT OF 1975

SEE Self-determination Policy.

INDIAN SELF-GOVERNMENT

SEE Governments, Native.

INDIAN TERRITORY

SEE Oklahoma.

INDIAN TRADE AND INTERCOURSE ACTS

The Indian Trade and Intercourse Acts were a series of acts passed between 1790 and 1834 that formed a large part of federal Indian policy. As the number of settlers grew, contact with tribes increased and problems emerged. The settlers intruded on Indian lands and took advantage of the Indians' unfamiliarity with land transactions to unfairly acquire more territory. The expanding non-Native civilization had a negative impact on tribes, and Indians suffered from poor treatment by European-Americans.

The government took action to protect Indians and to bring some means of justice to the relationship between tribes and settlers. The goal first was to centralize Indian policy under federal control. A secondary concern was to avoid possible extended Indian wars that would be expensive and financially draining for the newly formed country. The government created a policy to regulate interaction among Indians and non-Indians and to protect the tribes without preventing the mixing between the two races. The acts covered three basic policy areas: land transactions, trade with Indians, and handling crimes between Indians and non-Indians.

One of the primary objectives of the acts was to protect Indian landholdings and create bound-aries for Indian lands. Non-Indians were prohibited from purchasing land from individual Indians and tribes. Private treaties were invalid; lands could be acquired only under treaties in accordance with the U.S. Constitution. This included not only transactions with individual settlers, but also state and local governments. Non-Indians were prevented from settling on Indian lands and restricted from entering designated Indian Country areas. They could not graze animals or hunt within Indian lands. During one act revision, passports were required to enter Indian Country; however, this policy was later changed.

The acts created a procedure for licensing trading; to do business with Indians, traders had to be licensed by the U.S. government. Because Congress found greater need to protect Indians from unscrupulous traders and government agents, trade policy became more detailed in later acts. Later versions of the act prevented government employees working in Indian Affairs from having any special interest in Indian trade as additional protection from dishonesty.

The acts also contained measures covering criminal matters. It became a federal crime for a non-Indian to cause harm to an Indian or to engage in dishonest business practices. If convicted, the guilty party had to repay the damaged party as long as there was no attempt for private revenge. The act also awarded repayment to non-Indians for any harm done by Indians outside of designated Indian Country. The acts did not govern conduct of Native people among themselves; this was left up to the tribes.

There were four temporary acts passed between 1790 and 1799 before the first permanent act was passed in 1802. These temporary laws helped to revise and improve government policy before the first of the permanent acts was passed in 1802. The final permanent enactment was on June 30, 1834, the same day that the Department of Indian Affairs was created. The acts play an important part in the history of Indian legislation and policy, and the principles informing the acts form the basis for Indian law today.

SEE ALSO:

Indian Country; Indian New Deal (Indian Reorganization Act); Indian Policy, U.S.

INDIANA

Indiana became a U.S. state in 1816. The state has a long Indian history; sites around Indiana indicate that the Mound Builder civilization was active in Indiana hundreds of years ago. The largest Mound Builder site in the state is Angel Mound, which is located near present-day Evansville. The site was discovered and excavated starting in 1939, and nearly one million artifacts have been removed from the location.

The Indians' first contact with Europeans occurred in 1679, when Robert Cavelier, Sieur de La Salle, explored the Mississippi region and claimed it for France. The first permanent European settlement founded in Indiana was Vincennes, which was began in 1725 by French Jesuits.

From the time of European contact in 1679, many Indian tribes inhabited present-day Indiana. Initially, most were members of the Miami tribe, but throughout the 1700s and 1800s, they included members of the Lenape (Delaware), Mohican, Shawnee, Wyandot (Huron), Kickapoo, and Potawatomi peoples. The Potawatomis were the last tribe to enter and, in 1838, to leave the area.

Indiana contains no Indian reservations. The 1990 U.S. Census revealed that 12,720 Indiana residents were listed as American Indians, ranking Indiana thirty-third among U.S. states in terms of Native population.

SEE ALSO:
Miami; Mound Builders; Tecumseh.

INDIGENOUS PEOPLE (AS A TERM)

SEE American Indians; India; Native American.

INFANT DEATH RATE

The infant death rate for Indians, as reported by the Indian Health Service (IHS), is considerably higher than for non-Indians. From 1989 to 1991, the infant death rate for Indians was 12.0 for every 1,000 births, and the infant death rate among

This Apache baby is all smiles, but according to statistics gathered through 1991, a Native American baby's chances of surviving infancy are 30 percent less than those of a non-Native baby.

These Ak-Chin O'odham (Pima) children, no longer infants, have survived a dangerous period in the lives of Native people today.

non-Indians was 9.2 for every 1,000 births. This makes the Indian infant death rate 30 percent higher than that of other U.S. ethnic and racial groups.

As with most average figures, the higher average of infant deaths among Native people is affected by extremely high death rates in certain areas of the country. For example, recent figures show the Aberdeen IHS service population (located in the northern Great Plains) having an infant death rate of 17.5 for every 1,000 births. But figures for California show 4.8 deaths per 1,000 births, considerably lower than that of the Plains.

The IHS reports that 25 percent of infant deaths among Indians are caused by Sudden Infant Death Syndrome (SIDS), as compared with 14.1 percent for all other U.S. ethnic groups. According to the IHS, 21.8 percent of infant deaths among Native people are caused by congenital anomalies (birth defects). This compares with a rate of 21.5 percent for all other ethnic groups. Accidents and adverse effects are the cause of 6.1 percent of the infant deaths among Indians, and respiratory distress causes another 4.2 percent.

There are various reasons for the death rate among Indian infants being higher than for the general population. Some of the reasons are poor living conditions on Indian reservations and other areas with high Indian populations. Poverty conditions, poor sanitation, and hunger compound the death rate of American Indian infants.

SEE ALSO:
Indian Health Service.

INSTITUTE OF AMERICAN INDIAN ARTS

The Institute of American Indian Arts (IAIA) in Santa Fe, New Mexico, was founded by the Bureau of Indian Affairs in 1962. IAIA is the only institution of higher education exclusively devoted to the study and practice of American Indian and Alaskan Native art.

Having evolved out of a small Santa Fe arts studio headed by Dorothy Dunn in 1932, the institute has grown to include a student body of over two hundred people from twenty-nine states and seventy-seven tribes. Alumni and faculty are comprised of many distinguished Native American artists. The institute has been heralded as "a United Nation of Indian nations, a university within diversity . . . enriching, educational, broadening and exciting."

The institute offers fully accredited college courses toward associate of fine arts degrees, with future plans to expand to a four-year college program. Classes include painting, jewelry, ceramics, sculpture, filmmaking, and creative writing.

The Institute of American Arts Museum, established in 1972, grew out of a student honors program and through the help of donations from outside artists and private collectors. The museum holds a vast collection of contemporary paintings and over eight thousand sculptures, costumes, beadwork items, and photographs.

The collection records the thirty-year history of the institute and serves to inspire and encourage the institute's students, who benefit from the museum studies program with hands-on experience. The museum also is open to the public and serves to enhance an appreciation and awareness of the beauty and diversity of Native American artistic expression.

INUIT

The Inuit are the Native Arctic people who inhabit the coasts and inland areas of the Arctic and sub-Arctic regions of North America and the northeastern tip of Siberia. These Native people live in four countries—the United States (Alaska), Canada, Russia (Siberia), and Greenland.

Throughout this broad region, the Inuit are categorized according to location. The categories include the Alaskan Inuit, the Alaskan Yuit, and the Siberian Yuit. (Yuit is a term applied to the Inuit of Siberia and parts of Alaska.) Inuit who live on the coasts of southern Greenland are called Greenlanders or Kalaallitt and have taken on various European customs. In Canada, Natives who live on the coast opposite Newfoundland to Hudson Bay and on southern Baffin Island are known as Labrador Inuit. Those who live in the far northern regions of Greenland, on Baffin Island, and Hudson Bay are the Central Inuit. Natives who occupy Banks Island, Victoria Island, and other islands off the central Arctic coast are the Banks Island Inuit. The Mackenzie River Inuit live along the western Arctic coast of Canada.

This Inuit child in northwest Greenland is wearing a fox fur-trimmed hood for protection from the elements in the Arctic climate.

This display of Inuit sewing skill from Baffin Island in the Arctic also shows how some Inuits have incorporated Western religious ideas into their traditional cultures.

The Inuit were first called Eskimos ("eaters of raw flesh") by the Algonquian Indians, but they call themselves Inuit, a word that means "the people." Most anthropologists believe that they came to Arctic North America sometime after the arrival of the North American Indians, migrating across the Bering Strait to their new homeland. The oldest archaeological Inuit finds date from about 2000 B.C.E. and are located in southwestern Alaska and the Aleutian Islands.

Traditional Inuit families make their homes on cold, flat, barren lands. The family unit consists of the parents and their unmarried children plus any married sons and their wives and children. The head of the family is the oldest male who is still able to hunt. A group of families forms a settlement in winter, but in summer, the groups split up into the individual family units.

In Greenland and Alaska, villages consist of stone houses, while in Siberia, houses are made of driftwood and earth. Houses called igloos are made of various materials, including walrus or sealskin, depending on the season. *Igloo* is the Inuit word for "house." Snow blocks shaped into a dome form

the permanent winter housing for traditional Inuit people of central and eastern Canada.

The survival of traditional Inuit people in extremely harsh conditions is attributed to their ability to make tools, clothing, and housing from the materials at hand. The men hunt, fish, and build the housing, while women cook and make clothing. Their diet consists of seals, walrus, whales, fish, caribou, polar bears, foxes, hares, and seabirds, all of which may be frozen and eaten cooked or dried.

As in many societies that have kept the traditions and customs of their culture, ceremonies are performed prior to the hunt, and any animals that are killed are honored with rituals. Every part of the animal is used: Clothing, tents, and boats are made from the skins, while tools, needles, and weapons are made from the bones. The seal is the most valuable animal hunted by Inuit people and is used for food, fuel, and clothing. Seals also provide food for sled dogs and the raw materials used in making boats, harpoon lines, and tents.

Transportation methods of traditional Inuit people include the kayak, the umiak, and the dogsled.

An Inuit woman preparing fish in the Northwest Territories, Canada. Thanks to a claim settlement between the Inuit and the Canadian government, a new Inuit territory, called Nunavut, is to be formed in 1999.

These Inuit children are playing with toboggans on a snow-covered slope in northwest Greenland.

Resembling a canoe, the kayak holds one person who sits in a hole in the center of the boat. The craft is usually covered with sealskin or caribou skin and is used very successfully in hunting because it allows the hunter to move through the waters silently. The umiak, a large open boat, has a wooden frame covered with walrus hide. Large enough to carry people and goods, it is used to hunt in northern Alaska. The dogsled is usually made from wood and is pulled by as many as fourteen dogs. The dogsled is used both on land and frozen waterways. In modern times, methods of transportation also include motorized boats and snowmobiles.

The language of the Inuit constitutes a subfamily of the Eskimo-Aleut language family. There are differences in the languages of the Natives of Alaska according to whether the individuals identify themselves as Inuit or Yuit.

As a result of ever-increasing contact with the outside world, many Inuit people in Greenland, Siberia, Alaska, and Canada are slowly and steadily embracing present-day technology and customs. Today, many nontraditional Inuit people work for money, buy food from stores, and live in Western-type homes. Inuit people in Greenland have been influenced by the culture and customs of Denmark, while Inuit people of Siberia have been a part of planned political and social modernization by the former Soviet Union and present-day Russia since the 1930s. The Siberian Inuit hunt walrus, seals, and whales as a part of a collective today, instead of as individuals providing for their families.

The Inuit of Alaska lived a life that was relatively isolated from the outside world until the early to midpart of the twentieth century. The United States government then started to provide schools and medical services, although at a very minimal level. The exploitation of oil, gas, and other mineral supplies found in Alaska have greatly increased Inuit people's contact with the outside world, and many Alaskan Inuit people found employment on government construction projects. In recent times, Inuit people in Canada have also felt the encroachment of the outside world, particularly because of oil and mineral exploitation.

— B. Behm

SEE ALSO: